FINDING THE WAY

A Wanderer's Guide to Peace and Happiness in Christ

NELSON MENDES

WestBow
PRESS
A DIVISION OF THOMAS NELSON

Unless otherwise indicated, all Scripture quotations in this book are taken from *The New American Standard Bible (Canadian Edition, 1982)*. Copyright © 1960, 1962, 1963, 1968, 1971, 1972, 1975, 1977, 1995 by the Lockman Foundation. Used by permission (*www.lockman.org*).

Scriptures marked NIV are taken from *The Holy Bible, New International Version NIV*. Copyright © 1973, 1978, 1984 by International Bible Society. Used by Permission.

The names of individuals placed in quotation marks, and used in the author's personal stories in this book, are not their real names—they have been concealed for their privacy.

WestBow Press books may be ordered through booksellers or by contacting:

WestBow Press
A Division of Thomas Nelson
1663 Liberty Drive
Bloomington, IN 47403
www.westbowpress.com
1-(866) 928-1240

ISBN: 978-1-4497-3892-1 (hc)
ISBN: 978-1-4497-3890-7 (sc)
ISBN: 978-1-4497-3891-4 (e)
Library of Congress Control Number: 2012901741

Printed in the United States of America

WestBow Press rev. date: 02/07/2012

CONTENTS

INTRODUCTION xi

CHAPTER ONE   *Jesus: the Only Way* 1

CHAPTER TWO   *Jesus Christ, the God of Our Healing* 15

CHAPTER THREE   *Faith in Christ* 32

CHAPTER FOUR   *The Law and Prosperity* 44

CHAPTER FIVE   *Eternity* 51

CHAPTER SIX   *The Divide between Spirituality and Religion* 71

CHAPTER SEVEN   *Stress and Joy* 81

CHAPTER EIGHT   *Thy Kingdom Come* 101

AFTERWORD 107

ABOUT THE AUTHOR 109

To my grandmother, Matilde

I am a Hebrew, and I worship the Lord, the God of heaven, who made the sea and the land.

(The Book of Jonah, Verse 9, NIV)

INTRODUCTION

"And do not call *anyone* on earth your father; for
One is your Father, He who is in heaven.
And do not be called leaders; for One is your
Leader, *that is,* Christ" (Matthew 23: 9-10).

E ven though I live every breath and heartbeat in complete
faith in my Lord God and Savior Jesus Christ, this was
not always the case.

I was raised a Roman Catholic, went to a Catholic Separate
School, attended Mass every Sunday morning with my family,
and boy did I really know the Gospels, and the life of Jesus.
I had a moderate level of faith that Jesus was everything He
claimed to be, but as I became more immersed in the world,
my childlike curiosity and trust began to shift away from my
heart, and I began to live through my rational mind, my head.

I began to shape my identity around *me*—that success
and wealth in life came only by following the route set out by
successful, worldly people who came before me. Success to me
meant money, career, title, fame, perfect family, perfect place to
live, and the best toys the hand of man could craft.

Strangely enough, I didn't equate these things with
happiness, rather as the things we simply needed to possess, and
that contentment would somehow, randomly, appear. But in my
spiritual wandering, I eventually realized there is no denying
who you truly are in your heart; your feelings are always there

with you, and if you don't listen to them, you're deviating from your true self, your heart and soul. And when this happens, you've closed yourself off from God. No matter your situation, you need to remember to always listen to and be guided by your heart, rather than by the external approval of others.

Throughout high school and university, when I had ceased attending Mass, much to the extreme consternation of my religious mother (who is a spitting image of TV's *Judge Judy*, both in appearance, and in the ability to tongue lash you if you're doing something she disagrees with), I had solidified my position that I would live my life by science, reason, and logic alone. That all supernatural events, like the miracles worked by Jesus, were either all fabricated, or had a plausible, natural explanation, and were simply all exaggerations. In other words, if it couldn't be proven, then it didn't happen. But later on, for reasons I can't fully explain, I rediscovered Christ.

I had my doubts about writing and publishing this book because of what people would think of me, but then I cast the thought aside and said, "No. I believe in Jesus of Nazareth, and I have something positive to say. And if people laugh at me for sharing Him, then let them—the more, the better." And I was reminded by His encouragement:

> "Blessed are you when *men* revile you, and persecute you, and say all kinds of evil against you falsely, on account of Me. Rejoice, and be glad, for your reward in heaven is great, for so they persecuted the prophets who were before you" (Matthew 5: 11-12).

While I was ironing some clothes last year, I was listening to a radio program, and the talk show host was interviewing a university scholar about the validity of Jesus Christ in our modern world. This scholar began by saying that if Jesus were alive today He would be appalled as to what had become of Him, that He never wanted to be made into God—the Son of God—or to have had all these fictitious supernatural events, such as miracles and the resurrection from the dead, attributed to Him. He said that Jesus was not out to create a new religion, that He was a humanist who was simply trying to bring equality to the people of His day. And all the while this scholar was speaking I could feel the anger in his tone. Now I'm not disagreeing with him just because I'm Pentecostal Christian, and have Hebraic roots, but I am a student of history and the Bible, and I can say that this man was wrong in his point of view. And I'm not so sure he has read the New Testament from cover to cover.

Although we read in the Gospels that even His own family thought Jesus had lost His senses, it later became evident to those who were His witnesses that He was everything He said He was. Jesus clearly knew who He was, and made that repeatedly clear over and over again throughout the four Gospels. He said that He *is* the Christ (which means, "Messiah," or "Savior"), the Holy One and Son of God. Who He was, was the foundation of His ministry. So, on the one hand this scholar was accepting the social revolutionary aspects Jesus preached, yet discarded everything else about His existence that belongs to the realm of the religious or the supernatural.

I will admit that at one point I too struggled with the acceptance of His divine nature, but amongst other things, I was struck by the fact that Jesus' actions mirrored His words. That to accept Christ, I needed to accept *all* of what is written in the Gospels, or none of it at all. We don't have the luxury of being selective of what works for us, or what doesn't.

It was right around the same time that I was listening to another radio program documentary on the topic of Christian Evangelism in the Chinese Community here in Canada, and a Chinese man with weak English skills, but still understandable, began to relate of his experience when he was first introduced to Jesus of Nazareth.

He said that prior to immigrating to Canada, he lived most of his life in Communist ruled China, and had little to no concept of religion, let alone Christianity. What knowledge he had of it, was of it being a form of decadent Western propaganda, not unlike the free market economy.

When he was invited to read the Bible in Chinese by friends of his, he could barely believe what he was hearing. He said he was overwhelmed, and began sobbing because the words of Jesus were so beautiful. And I could sense his giddiness and emotion over the radio while he recounted his experience. He said he could scarcely believe that such a wonderful treasure had existed all this time, and that he had spent his whole life in ignorance of it. He said he accepted Jesus as his Lord and Savior that very hour, and has dedicated the rest of his life to following His teachings. His heart had in fact found the "kingdom of heaven" that Jesus so often described in His parables:

> "The kingdom of heaven is like a treasure hidden in the field, which a man found and hid; and from joy over it he goes and sells all that he has, and buys that field" (Matthew 13:44).

And the account of his discovery of Christ was so profound, that for a second (and only for a second), I felt somewhat embarrassed for not having the same sense of daily devotion for being a Christian.

I have spent considerable time studying world religions for the past number of years, partly because I had not *fully* embraced Jesus at the time, and also because I knew that if we are to compare our own belief systems with those of others, it is a good idea to be a cultural tourist, to see how others live. And I have respect for all religious faiths that promote peace and goodwill. In places that have not come to know Christ, their cultural traditions have evolved in adaptation to their given environments, and their beliefs have worked for them as best they could. And although I do not agree with their theologies, nevertheless, their pursuit of cultivating a good heart does have merit.

So for me personally, I believe there is only *one* true way—that which was confirmed in the life of Jesus of Nazareth. But when Jesus directed His disciples to spread the "Good News" to all the ends of the earth, He wasn't suggesting that it be forced upon anyone. We best reflect the nature of Christ by how we devote and live our lives according to His teachings. When you commit your life to following Jesus, you'll need nothing else as the center-point of your existence. All the great spiritual masters have faintly echoed the example of Jesus, so why not go directly to the source Himself? The more I study the Gospels, I become more deeply amazed, and even *more* aware of the truth He represented. Jesus not only reminded us to live upright lives and to love one another, but to me, He confirmed that what He said was true by His actions—He proved that He is Deity.

However, before accepting Christ into my life, my rational mind began juggling the story of His life in the Gospels, and all the information and artefacts that it could find to convince me that Jesus was who He said He was; *something* was working within me, pushing me to go back to my early fascination with Him when I was growing up.

I looked at the unchanging nature of human behavior, and couldn't get over the fact that several of Christ's apostles, those who walked with Him during His mission on Planet Earth, were tortured and killed because of their conviction of what they had witnessed. Why now would anyone subject themselves to being killed if what they knew to be true was in fact a complete fabrication? Simon Peter, who would become the first Pope of the Roman Catholic Church, was apparently crucified upside down (because as tradition has it, "he was not worthy to die as Jesus had died"). Others were stoned to death and beheaded, among other brutal methods of execution. I truly do not believe that anyone would submit themselves to persecution and death out of a sense of guilt or obligation to someone. Something *very real* and profound was at work in the beliefs of the men and women who knew Jesus.

The Shroud of Turin, which I believe to be the genuine burial cloth of Jesus, has captivated me since I watched an early television documentary of its public scientific analysis. It bears the image of a man who had been tortured and crucified. It is in fact better than a photograph, in that it is literally a time capsule of a massive amount of physical and visual material from its time. I'm not going to go into a detailed discussion or debate concerning it, as there are those who don't believe it bears the authentic image of Jesus, while others think it to be a masterful forgery (perhaps even created by Leonardo da Vinci himself). I can only say that the following general scientific observations really struck me as corroboration of the proof of the account of Christ's Passion (trial and crucifixion) in the Gospels.

From a morphological, or physical standpoint, the man appears to be racially Hebrew; there are (nail) piercings in the wrists and feet, typifying death by Roman crucifixion, or in other words, being nailed to a wooden cross; there is a chest wound matching the spear thrust by the Roman soldier to confirm that Jesus was dead; there are puncture wounds around the top of the man's head, matching the crown of thorns mockingly placed upon Jesus' head; there are scourge marks across the body which resemble the Roman whip used in the first century AD; the linen burial cloth dates to the same period in which Jesus lived (there was a dispute over its age several years ago because a carbon dating test came up with an age of about eight hundred years. However, it was recently shown that the cloth fibers used for the test were ones that were rewoven into the Shroud in order to conserve it during the Middle Ages); there are microscopic rock particles on the Shroud which are specific to Jerusalem; residual images of several species of flowers indigenous to Jerusalem were found imprinted on the Shroud (it appears they were placed upon Jesus by His mourners); the imprint of the Hebrew word, "Abba" (which means, "Father, or "Daddy") has been identified directly beneath the man's chin. This was likely a small plaque that was placed there at the time of entombment; physicists have noted background radiation (gamma rays) being inexplicably emitted from the Shroud. There is the belief that an energy burst occurred that fused the blood, sweat and grime that covered the man, into the fibers of the burial cloth, leaving evidence of what one scientist called a singularity, an event horizon. In other words, from a spiritual viewpoint, a "miracle." And the discoveries keep getting deeper with greater technological advances and analysis.

To me, this is merely Jesus speaking to us through the ages, saying, "As when I walked the byways of Judea, people sought signs, proof. You are no different. So here is a small gift to help you believe, and to bolster the faith of those who already believe in Me." Although I embraced Jesus as the Messiah when I was "born again," nevertheless, I appreciated the added certainty of the revelations of the Shroud of Turin, to at least put my ever-questioning mind at ease. And if Jesus wasn't who He said He was, then what was the point of it all?

Ask yourself, what gives you joy, and what gives you the fuel to wake up with energy every morning? Do you have a good relationship with others and yourself, or is something missing? Jesus came to save the lost. He came to heal the broken-hearted, and to show us that there is a lot more to our existence than what we may think.

Look beyond existing dogma, and always pursue your dreams, and grow the power of your imagination. For we have two lives—our waking life, and the life of our dreams and imagination. And how real do your dreams feel to you? I don't know about you, but they can seem quite solid and indistinguishable from real life sometimes. That is, we have an aspect of ourselves that we know is intangible, yet very real. In fact, research has shown that our limbic mind (the part of the brain that regulates emotion) cannot distinguish between what is real, and what is imagined. This is why so many athletes, in particular, do visualization training, practicing their moves and plays before actually engaging in the real thing. And do you know what happens? The brain follows through on these simulated sessions as if it was familiar with the routines, thereby creating greater confidence and completion. In other words, this is where reality and imagination intersect. So the question that you as an unbeliever have to ask yourself, is how do you want to explain your existence—by things you can *only* define with your five senses, or take that leap of faith, that in addition to the world your powers of physical perception can detect, there is another, broader, deeper existence all around us? How could it not be so?

Just take a look at our vision. Our eyes can only see a small fraction of the electromagnetic spectrum—we see white light, composed of the colors of the rainbow. However, we can't see the way a lot of other creatures see, such as in infrared or ultraviolet. And yet we know that another visual universe sits right in front of us. And there is that "other sense" that science has a hard time with—the "sixth sense," intuition. This is certainly another level of engagement that our spirit uses to see into that deeper reality that surrounds us.

Our lives and this vast universe that we live in are not the acts of random chance—there is an intelligent Creator who has a plan for us and all things. So we need to pray and cast aside our doubt, and be bold in our requests, knowing that there *is* a benevolent God who will grant everything we need. Jesus reminded us to always walk in faith, and not give in to the ignorance of the world, whose "wisdom" is so short-sighted, and lacking.

—Nelson Mendes

CHAPTER ONE

Jesus: the Only Way

"For the Father loves the Son, and shows Him all things that He Himself is doing; and greater works than these will He show Him, that you may marvel" (John 5: 20).

Don't ask me why, but that morning before heading off to work when I turned on the stereo radio, instead of tuning in to the local news and weather like I normally did, I turned the dial until I heard the next clear broadcast coming through on the airwaves. It was a preacher talking about being baptized by the Holy Spirit, and how we needed to be born again in Jesus Christ to receive the gift of eternal life.

I was looking out the front window at the passing cars while sipping my coffee, and I rolled my eyes and grumbled, "Born again. What's that supposed to mean, anyways? Ridiculous. Meaningless jargon only a gun-toting, beer guzzling, pickup truck-driving, ignorant redneck would use to claim some sense of direction in his small life."

I walked back over to the radio and turned off the theological rant. The house became dead silent, and the noise of the traffic had ceased outside. I took a few steps, but I suddenly froze, and could feel a warm and growing sensation deep in my chest, in my heart. I wasn't worried because it didn't hurt, but I knew it wasn't the coffee that was generating this flame within me. My brain struggled to grasp at what was happening. It was confused because the feeling was entirely outside of my comprehension.

I sat down on the couch, and I quietly asked myself, "What is this?" But I immediately began to realize what it was. I was being born again.

I felt a profound mixture of joy, warmth, peace, and complete understanding of Jesus. It was like liquid love swirling in my heart and my entire being, as if every cell and fiber of my body were fully awake and aware of Him at a deeply personal level.

This lasted no more than a minute, and it then dissipated, and was gone. But the memory of the experience has never left me. My inner vision shifted that day, and I began walking a new spiritual path.

THE ETERNAL AND FAITHFUL GUIDE

Do you ever wonder about the meaning of your life? Do you ever ask yourself, "Is there a purpose for me?" If you are at a crossroads in your life, then that's okay! It just means that your soul, your heart—that part of your true self—is trying to get your attention. In other words, God is speaking to you through your heart. God is seeking to put you back on the path of fulfilling your destiny.

Now don't be angry with me when I say this, especially if you're going through some difficult times, but you were made to be perfect and to live a life of joy and abundance. A perfect God would not have created anything less! The problem is that most of us have not only lost touch with God, but with ourselves.

So, essentially, we're wandering in the woods, and we're lost—we've wandered off the marked hiking trail. And what are ways we can get back to the trail? Well, we can try to retrace our steps, we can holler to see if someone hears us, or we can pull out some tools we might have with us, such as a trail map, or a compass. In the end, had we had a guide, we would have never gone off course in the first place.

Fortunately for us, we have the greatest trail map, compass, GPS, and seasoned guide that has ever been, or will ever be—He is Jesus Christ. And when He is front and center in your life, every step you take will be filled with confidence and security.

For Christians who already believe in Jesus, I encourage you to continue in deepening your relationship with Him. For those of you who do not have faith in Him, then this very moment is your opportunity. And when I say "believe," I don't just mean believing that what He said are nice things to live by, but to fully embrace Him as the living Son of God, who overcame the world, and conquered all ignorance, sickness, and even death itself. Jesus was not simply an historical figure who walked the shores of the Sea of Galilee two thousand years ago. He is an eternal, loving, spiritual being who is alive in the here and now, and always with those who seek Him out. This realization is something which will transcend your rational mind. Your acceptance of Jesus will occur deep within your heart at a level where words will completely escape you. Your awareness will not be informational, but true, personal, knowledge. I encourage you to get a copy of the New Testament (or a copy of the Bible that has both the Old and New Testaments), and read the Gospels written by the Four Evangelists, Matthew, Mark, Luke and John. See not only what Jesus said, but what He *did* to prove who He was, and the meaning of His three and a half year ministry.

His life and teachings are the most complete guide book for living a rich and abundant life available to us. In following it, we follow Him. And in doing so faithfully, we can never go wrong.

THE MASTER CARPENTER'S TOOL KIT—THE GIFTS AND TEACHINGS OF CHRIST

Of the many titles that Jesus has been given, such as "King of Kings," "The Good Shepherd," and "Prince of Peace," He was a very practical and grounded person who lived a life as a carpenter before He embarked on His ministry. Jesus was already accustomed to the fact that without the proper tools and training, the job could not get done; so too with living an abundant life in relationship with God. Without the right life skills, we cannot craft the plans and build the life that we desire.

ATTITUDE

I'd say above all else, Jesus challenged us to change our attitude to things in our life—to think boldly and positively in overcoming obstacles. Without this mindset, little else is possible.

It has been said that ninety-eight percent of our thoughts and behavior are the same ones we've had the day before! No wonder things don't seem to improve in our lives. Even a small shift in our thinking can begin to have noticeable daily effects.

There is nothing worse than being stuck, whether it's in an elevator or having your car trapped in a snowdrift. So too with our thoughts, especially when they're keeping us in the same, uneventful and unfulfilling situation. Even the great physicist, Albert Einstein, said that imagination is more important than knowledge. Why? Because existing knowledge says, "This is all that we know, so this is what you need to base your life on." But unless we shift our thinking—change our attitude and *open up our imagination*—new discoveries can never be made. This is what Jesus meant when He said:

"Nor do men put new wine into old wineskins; otherwise the wineskins burst, and the wine pours out, and the wineskins are ruined; but they put new wine into fresh wineskins, and both are preserved" (Matthew 9:17).

We must change how we perceive things ("new wine") so that we can change who we are ("new wineskins"). *And how exactly do we go about putting new wine into new wineskins? Easier said than done*, you've likely already thought. Well, I like to think of it this way. It all comes down to changing our habits and creating new ones. And you definitely can't tell me you don't know what a habit is, or what habits you have.

Habits are so automatic that we're not aware of them most of the time. That's because they act like computer programs in our subconscious mind, doing things behind the scenes without our conscious awareness. Scientists who study the brain have demonstrated that roughly ninety-five percent of our behavior is controlled by our subconscious mind, while the remaining five percent is regulated by our conscious thinking. Staggering, isn't it? And these numbers are quite close to the previous figure of our thoughts being the same from day to day. Quite the rut we can get ourselves into, right? But on the flip side, we can use this fact to our advantage.

We can change our habits into ones that empower us, rather than keeping us stuck in unhappy circumstances. The key to creating new and empowering behavior is how we think. We can use that five percent of conscious control to transform our entire reality.

WORDS

"But the things that proceed out of the mouth come from the heart, and those defile the man. For out of the heart come evil thoughts, murders, adulteries, fornications, thefts, false witness, slanders" (Matthew 15: 18-19).

How then do we go about changing our thoughts, which then change our habits? We do this by being *conscious* of the words we think and say both to ourselves and to others.

As Jesus said in the above verse, it is the words that come out of us that defile or diminish us. That is, if our words are pessimistic and lack hope, then we literally become what we say. Words shape our reality because they possess meaning. Therefore, we truly need to be mindful of what we think and say. So instead of having a thought like, *I'm never going to succeed*, affirm to yourself, *Yes, I believe, and I'm certain that I will succeed!* This is what you want to sink into your subconscious in order to direct your actions during the day.

Really start to examine the words that come to mind and leave your mouth every day. What are they like? Are they positive, or are they words that are less than inspiring? Try asking a co-worker, friend or family member what your language is like. What's good about it, or what's not? You might be surprised how automatic and repetitive your negative speech is. So, by being aware of these words, you can now begin to stop saying them, and replace them with motivating ones.

WORDS CAN KILL, AND WORDS CAN BRING LIFE

"And when he had said these things, He cried out with a loud voice, 'Lazarus, come forth.' He who had died came forth, bound hand and foot with wrappings; and his face was wrapped around with a cloth. Jesus said to them, 'Unbind him, and let him go'" (John 11: 43-44).

The wrong words can kill your dreams and your future. But the right words can give you new life and establish your prosperity. So fill your heart with the best words possible and truly feel their power when they enter your mind and they leave your tongue. Ultimately, it's about how you feel and how you make others feel. When in doubt about the impact of your words, simply don't use them.

I am deeply saddened whenever I hear that a young person has taken their life because of having been bullied over the Internet, such as on Facebook or other social media networks. When I went to school, the only bullies we had to contend with were in the schoolyard, and the saying, "Sticks and stones may break my bones, but names will never hurt me" was used as a brave defence. Mind you, this rarely deterred bullies from using verbal abuse and muscle to inflict pain. Sadly, this old kid's saying was probably never true for the part about "names will never hurt me" back then, and especially not now. We must all take full responsibility not only within our homes, but in our media, to focus our attention at preventing the use of language that hurts.

Begin to apply these principles in your life and you'll begin to see the reality of who Jesus is and the spirit that moves through you. Like Jesus said to Nicodemus,

> "The wind blows where it wishes and you hear the sound of it, but do not know where it comes from and where it is going; so is everyone who is born of the Spirit." (John 3: 8)

PRAYER

> "And in the early morning, while it was still dark, He arose and went out and departed to a lonely place, and was praying there" (Mark 1: 35).

7

Prayer changes lives and changes circumstances. And we know that in our words are power, life and death. So when we pray to Jesus, we can be certain that our words are not being used in vain.

You have probably heard this already, but I'll say it again: prayer is the greatest power available to us to effect change and transformation in our lives. When done with sincerity and in complete faith, we open our heart and the communication lines to the holy. We suspend our reasoning mind that is governed by limitations, and switch gears to a mind, and "heartset," that are open to unlimited possibility. When our prayers and intentions are aligned with the will of God, then they will be made manifest.

Jesus was a prayer warrior—He set the standard for how we should pray. Take time to pray every day, or whenever you feel your heart tells you to. When done in a state of expectation and hope, you should notice greater confidence and a bit of an extra bounce in your step. The key is to not let doubt creep in.

Doubt is the greatest way to neutralize your hope and can derail you. In observing how Jesus conducted Himself, there was absolutely no doubt in Him whatsoever. He knew that whatever He requested would come true and be made real. For He reminded us:

> "Truly I say to you, whoever says to this mountain, 'Be taken up and cast into the sea,' and does not doubt in his heart, but believes that what he says is going to happen, it shall be *granted* him" (Mark 11: 23).

There have been numerous times when I've been made aware of people who have been sick, and where I've told their loved ones that I'd pray for them. They'd often look at me like I had just said that *Batman* was a real person, and these were Churchgoers no less! Sometimes they'd blurt out, "Well, I've always prayed, and it doesn't work for me," or "God doesn't hear my prayers," and so on. First of all, that kind of attitude won't get you anywhere. And secondly, I would say that they were not in right relationship with God. If you doubt God can deliver, then more than likely, you doubt that He even exists at all. We must be persistent! Jesus stressed that we need to "keep at it," to never give up, as in the following parable:

> "There was a certain judge who did not fear God, and did not respect man.
>
> And there was a widow in that city, and she kept coming to him, saying, 'Give me legal protection from my opponent'.
>
> And for a while he was unwilling; but afterward he said to himself, 'Even though I do not fear God nor respect man, yet because this widow bothers me, I will give her legal protection, lest by continually coming she wear me out.'
>
> And the Lord said, "Hear what the unrighteous judge said;
>
> Now shall not God bring about justice for His elect, who cry to Him day and night, and will He delay long over them? I tell you that He will bring about justice for them speedily" (Luke 18: 2-8).

When looking for strength and guidance, pray these words:

> *Jesus, You are my Lord and my Savior, and I am nothing without You. Please give me strength and guidance in every moment of every day. Amen.*

I'm often asked if we should pray to God, or to Jesus, and if there is any difference? Personally, I mostly pray to Jesus, as He is *also* God—God the Son, and He said that whenever we pray to Him, He will be our advocate to God the Father, ensuring our prayers are delivered. Remember, they are two divine and infinite beings from whom all goodness flows to us from heaven. But you may pray directly to God as Jesus did. It is a matter of how you are guided to pray in the spirit.

RELATIONSHIP

Prayer isn't strictly about seeking something we genuinely need in our lives, but it's about fostering our relationship with God. We acknowledge that alone, we are not as strong as when He is with us. Although it is important to rely on other people and their expertise, ultimate healing or assistance comes from God. We can never lose sight of this. Jesus reminded us that God is our Father, and that He will look after us and provide for us:

> "If you then being evil, know how to give good gifts to your children, how much more shall *your* Heavenly Father give the Holy Spirit to those who ask Him?" (Luke 11: 13).

And why does He provide for us? Because He loves us. And how can we receive anything unless we have a relationship with Him? Is it not easier to receive assistance from a family member or a friend than it is from a complete stranger? Like any relationship, the more you devote to it, the stronger and deeper it will become. That is why praying sincerely from the heart instils our confidence in God to become second-nature. We move from a position of uncertainty, to one of trust.

There is no fooling yourself if you speak to God with empty words—you'll feel hollow and see prayer as a chore rather than something you genuinely look forward to. How you pray isn't what's important. It's your intent that counts. We each have our own style, so just do what feels most comfortable for you. Whether you pray in silence in bed, on your knees, or in the shower, remember that God weighs your heart and does not judge you by your outward appearance. Jesus spent a considerable amount of time pointing out our need to be authentic, and to stop being a "fake" in our faith like the Scribes and Pharisees of His day:

> "Even so you too outwardly appear righteous to men, but inwardly you are full of hypocrisy and lawlessness" (Matthew 23: 28).

Back when I was a volunteer at Parkwood Hospital in London (Ontario) in the 1990s as a means to enhance my curriculum vitae with community service credentials, I discovered the importance of being authentic in our faith and motives.

Parkwood is a hospital dedicated to caring for chronically ill patients with Multiple sclerosis (MS) and other degenerative diseases, as well as physical rehabilitation from accidents. There is also a large contingent of retired military veterans who call it home.

My role was to transport patients from their rooms every Sunday morning so they could attend Church service in the hospital gymnasium. Other volunteers attended to bringing Roman Catholics down to Mass in the hospital chapel.

There were some really sad cases of younger adults, in particular, who had become so disabled, that their families could no longer look after them at home, and had placed them under the hospital's care.

It was my first day of duty as a transporter, and I entered the room of one my first transportees and a strange sensation came over me, as if I were walking through a "bubble of peace." I don't know how else to describe it, but my energy level went up several notches. Sitting before me in her wheelchair was a very pretty woman with short, salt and pepper hair, and she was very neatly dressed. My guess was that she was in her mid 40s.

I kindly said good morning to "Susan," but she was completely motionless. I don't know exactly what she was suffering from, but I believe it was Lou Gehrig's disease. She did, however, manage to make eye contact with me, and her dark eyes were shining. I understood that she was saying, "Hello."

As I went behind her to begin pushing the wheelchair, I saw her family photo. There she was in healthier days with her husband and her two young daughters. Surrounding the picture frame where several little stuffed toy animals, no doubt from her kids. I could tell they loved her dearly. My heart began to break. I paused for a few moments, then regained my composure and shuttled her down to Church.

The other volunteers on my team had been just as busy getting their charges down to the service, and soon we had a full house. Several rows of parked wheelchairs cradling the old and the young, broken in body, but not in spirit, were ready to hear words of hope from the visiting pastor.

A couple of songs were sung to start things off, and those who were still able to use their vocal chords joined in. I had pulled up a chair to sit beside Susan. As we began singing, *What a Friend We Have in Jesus*, she lit right up. She was humming the lyrics, and swaying slightly from side-to-side—she was so happy.

Even in the midst of her condition, her faith is so strong! I marvelled. I felt so small and pathetic for being the seriously flawed person that I was. I was young and healthy, and yet here I was doing this for selfish reasons. And I felt hollow for not having the faith that she possessed.

After I had taken her back to her room, her eyes were glowing, or rather, she was glowing. As I said good-bye to her, I knew that no words were necessary to describe how grateful Susan was for having been taken to worship service, and for being alive.

Jesus wanted us to realize that all those things that impede or hinder us can be removed by faith, and that we could live life abundantly. This includes living at peace with our neighbor, both within our immediate community, and globally.

So why is there so much strife and conflict in the world? Because we're not in relationship with God and ourselves. Sound familiar? Greed and self-centeredness, or what some modern psychologists would call, "living through the egoic mind," create walls of separation between us. The egoic mind is our belief that we matter more than anyone else, that we need to accumulate money, power, titles, trophies, and objects for our own happiness and security, and that we have acquired success through the labor of our own efforts. This false realization only ever contributes to an inner feeling of emptiness, if not private suffering.

I would argue, as Jesus did, that peace comes through serving others. By putting others first, we will be rewarded and glorified:

"Give, and it will be given to you; good measure pressed down, shaken together, running over, they will pour into your lap. For whatever measure you deal out to *others*, it will be dealt to you in return" (Luke 6: 38).

And in all of your work, no matter what your position or job title is, focus first on the service you are providing, and lastly on the pay or the reward you are getting. And always serve in God's name.

How have you felt whenever someone opened a door for you, or when you did the same and were graciously thanked for it? What do you think was being exchanged between you? Could you feel it? Was it not *love*? For in helping others, we are loving them, and God. There is nothing less.

Before I moved from Ontario to work in downtown Calgary, Alberta, the metropolis of Canada's fast paced petroleum industry, I was a Petroleum Landman in Southern Ontario acquiring oil and gas leases from farmers in order to drill oil and gas wells on their land. Whenever driving down a country road, I'd always be waved at, even if the farmer riding his John Deere tractor knew me or not. I would, of course, smile and wave back. I always remember how good I felt with that exchange. Had I waved to someone while driving to work in Calgary, they'd assume I knew them, or if not, they'd be utterly confused, if not downright suspicious, because nobody waves to anyone in a big city if they have no business with them. Okay, well it may not be all that convenient to be saying hello to hundreds of people who cross your path in a big city, but even having a smile on your face, or a thoughtful expression to someone you pass along the sidewalk, is like saying hello to them. And trust me, I've walked past far too many people who I could have sworn were zombies—there was an empty, hollow look to them.

Just as Jesus expects us to have a relationship with Him, so He expects us to have one with others by the way we carry ourselves, and to acknowledge our neighbors as being children of God like ourselves.

CHAPTER TWO

Jesus Christ,
the God of Our Healing

"And wherever He entered villages, or cities, or countryside, they were laying the sick in the market places, and entreating Him that they might just touch the fringe of His cloak; and as many as touched it were being cured" (Mark 6: 56).

Diseases of every form imaginable are some of the greatest impediments to our happiness and wellbeing, and they affect us all. Some are brief, but others linger or come and go. For those who suffer from a serious or chronic illness, it can be no less than living in your own private state of hell.

But why do we get ill in the first place? Some illnesses can be readily explained, while others seem to elude us. Medical science, on the whole, has worked diligently to reduce human suffering, but there is still much to be done.

I am confident that no one suffers from a disease because of some form of punishment from God. In Jesus' day, there was the belief that children could inherit the sins of their parents in the form of sickness:

> "And as He passed by, He saw a man blind from
> birth. And His disciples asked Him, saying, "Rabbi,
> who sinned, this man or his parents, that he should
> be born blind?"
>
> Jesus answered, "*It was neither that* this man
> sinned, nor his parents; but *it was* in order that the
> works of God might be displayed in him" (John
> 9: 1-3).

Now when we talk about sin, it means "missing the mark" of correct conduct. That is, breaking the commandments of God. The religious authorities of ancient Israel were continually pointing out sins and offences of the Jewish people to the point that it became a crushing burden of guilt to most. Jesus criticized the extreme legalism of His day and worked to cut through the red tape of the law to get to the heart of those who were suffering.

Look at your own situation, or of someone close to you. Are you made to feel guilty about a certain behavior you have? Perhaps ask someone who is clinically obese and is made to feel guilty for being overweight, or someone who has developed lung cancer because of their addiction to smoking and nicotine. Whatever the disease may be, we should not engage in judgment and criticism. Those who are in pain require our prayers, assistance, and compassion.

Jesus understood that healing began at the level of the heart. And in healing the heart, the mind and body were subsequently healed. One thing that greatly irritated the religious authorities was when Jesus forgave sins, guilt. To the Pharisees, this was blasphemy, for they argued only God could forgive sins. But ultimately, they preferred to see the masses live in guilt so they could continue to dominate them and keep them down.

Look at your own life. Is there someone or something holding you down? Is it possible that you, yourself, are the one keeping you captive? And what is creating or adding to the suffering? Is it a false concept or belief? Sometimes we simply can't identify what the root cause of our discomfort is. In these instances, we need to pray to Jesus to reveal to our hearts that which we cannot see so that we can be liberated from the bondage of our disease. This doesn't mean ignoring medical treatment—by all means, we need to work with doctors and healthcare practitioners as part of our overall strategy. But we also need to go into ourselves and open our heart to Christ to maximize our recovery.

In my own experience, I've observed that the source of many ailments revolve around how we judge others, and ourselves. For example, whenever you think of someone whom you dislike, what happens? Do you not repeat the same thought pattern and have the same feelings as if you'd picked up a familiar book and began reading it over again? In a way, you're reinforcing the negative relationship you have with them in your heart, even though they may live far away from you, or in fact, may have already long since died.

Now let us shift from the level of feeling and thought to what happens in your body, because your emotional health directly impacts your physical health.

Several years ago, I read a book by Deepak Chopra called, *Ageless Body, Timeless Mind*, and I was captivated by how our endocrine system (or our glandular system) reacts to our thoughts and emotions to create biochemical messengers in our bodies. Without getting into a detailed scientific explanation, the essence of the book is that we are what we think. If we have happy, loving thoughts, then we produce molecules that make and keep us healthy. If we have negative thoughts, then we produce molecules that can make us sick, and keep us sick.

I will be the first one to admit that my judgment of people, especially those I'd never met, truly needed changing. And it took a huge conscious effort to undo my robotic, habitual, thinking.

I was walking to the office one morning and an obese man passed me on the sidewalk, and I remember thinking to myself, *Wow, why doesn't that guy lay off on the potato chips?* I walked a few more steps realizing the significance of what I had just said to myself, and I stopped dead in my tracks. I was actually shocked. And I thought, *Where on Earth did THAT come from? And what right on God's blue planet do I have to think that of another human being? How do I know what sort of struggles and difficulties that person might be going through? And, what if I was in some mishap, and that individual ended up saving my life?* And, of course, I embarrassingly thought, *Jesus would never have allowed that to cross His mind!*

I swore from that moment on, that I would be mindful of my negative impressions of others. And boy, did it take work! I understood that I had to start reprogramming my subconscious mind so that instead of "garbage" coming into my head, good things did.

Also, I began to reflect on the fact that our judgment of others isn't really a true reflection of our soul—that it comes from the level of fear, and ignorance—from the egoic mind. Judgment creates separation, which can then lead to anger, and then to hatred. Indeed, is this not at the root of most of the world's troubles?

I surmised that every time I had a critical concept of someone, unhealthy molecules were being created and released in my body, thereby diminishing my vitality. And how sick can a person become if they think like this all day long? Can you imagine how much productive brain space we can harness from eliminating these unconstructive patterns?

Jesus warned us to be conscious of our judgmental attitude. In other words, to stop being hypocrites:

> "And why do you look at the speck in your brother's eye, but do not notice the log that is in your own eye?" (Matthew 7:3).

So, needless to say, I prayed that the Holy Spirit—*the invisible, transformative agency and power of God*—would work within me to make me aware of all my intentions, thoughts, words, and actions. Then I began to put my intent into practice. For example, the next time I passed someone on the street, instead of me thinking, *That person has a weird nose*, I would consciously think, *That person has a "unique" nose.* Or in place of, *That person is so short they probably can't see over their car dashboard*, I would think, *God made that person perfect just the way they are.*

Through my revelation, rather than feeling guilty or beating myself up over my hypocritical behavior, I acknowledged the fact that the majority of us are in the same predicament, and that this was my chance to make a fundamental and lasting change in my life for the better. So I challenge you to do the same, because slowly, you will begin to notice that your mind will be freed up to pursuing things you enjoy, and you will feel healthier and more energetic.

STOP JUDGING YOURSELF TOO

Not only can we feel unwell when we think of someone we don't get along with, or can't relate to, but also in the way we self-obsess over ourselves, or negatively view who we are. We can be subjected to enough abuse by others if we allow it, so why would we turn on ourselves as well? Whatever your situation is, don't ever call yourself downgrading names, or foster any behavior that makes you think that someone else is somehow better than you are, because it is simply not true. God created us all as equals. Just because someone is "wealthier," "better looking," or has "a better job" than you, does not mean they have a greater right to walk the earth and breathe the air than you do.

Don't buy into the collective consciousness of the world where corporations influence us to look and act in a certain way. Trust me, they're thinking primarily of the money they can make from you if you buy that sporty new car, smart phone, or designer pair of jeans. Walk in your own footsteps, along the path that Jesus set out for us, and liberate yourself from feelings of guilt and inadequacy.

This is not to say that pursuing "stuff" is wrong, only how you relate to it, and how it determines your self-image. You don't need to be accepted by a status-driven world—Jesus has already accepted you just the way you are. So respect and honor yourself always.

Also, remember that no matter what difficulty you are going through, you're likely not the only one going through the same experience—suffering is not exclusive to you. Too often we forget that the planet does not solely revolve around us, and in fact, there is always someone in greater need than we are. Have you ever turned a small body ache into something more that what it really was, thereby "adding fuel to the fire"? Try shifting your focus away from yourself every so often, and think about helping someone, no matter how insignificant you might think that assistance is.

FORGIVENESS AND BLESSING

I have briefly referred to sin as it relates to holding onto guilt, and although we're likely not reminded of sin on a daily basis as the Jews of Jesus' time were, nevertheless, we need to continually scrutinize our conduct for its purity, or lack thereof. We need to get serious about sin. Aside from the fact that it contravenes God's laws, it inflicts emotional damage upon us and others. If you are carrying around guilt that prevents you from sleeping at night, or looking yourself in the mirror, then this can cause great harm to your spiritual, emotional, and biological wellbeing. You need to face this sin head-on as soon as possible, because time will not erase it, rather it will only linger and fester within you.

Forgiveness is a very powerful spiritual tool in lifting us out of illness because it undoes that emotional blockage that we may be holding within us. Namely, our heart is freed of this unseen, yet very real, burden. And forgiveness is a cornerstone of the Lord's Prayer which Jesus taught to His disciples:

"Our Father who art in heaven,
Hallowed be Thy name.
Thy kingdom come.
Thy will be done,
On earth as it is in heaven.
Give us this day our daily bread.
And forgive us our trespasses, as we forgive those who trespass against us.
And lead us not into temptation, but deliver us from evil.
For Thine is the kingdom, and the power, and glory, forever, and ever. Amen" (Matthew 6: 9-13).

REFLECTION

We all know whether we've said or done something to harm someone because we possess a conscience. And upon reflecting upon the day we've had, we can use it as an opportunity to improve ourselves and polish up on our behavior.

One thing I try to do every night before going to bed is to reflect upon those things I may have said or done during the day that I could have handled better. I ask God for His forgiveness and for the clarity of mind to not repeat my behavior again. If the offense is of a scale that merits approaching the person I've offended (either knowingly, or unknowingly), then I'd approach the co-worker, friend, or family member the next day and ask for their forgiveness. Many times, the burden we carry is solely our own, because the words or actions we may have performed may not in fact have been viewed negatively by the ones we thought we had offended. Either way, it is better to clear your conscience rather than being uncertain if you had caused harm or not.

For strangers you may not have been nice to, such as that door-to-door salesperson you were rude to, and whom you'll likely never see again, still ask God to forgive you. The key here is not to have yourself walking on eggshells fearing everything that may come out of your mouth, but to be genuinely mindful of your ways, rather than acting in an unconscious way that may have gotten you into trouble in the past.

"Okay, time out," you're telling me. "Why should I feel guilty of having offended, or sinned, against "so-and-so" if they were a jerk to me? I'm only paying them back what they deserved." Herein lies the radical shift Jesus demanded that we make to our heart and soul concerning our relationship with others. When asked what the greatest commandment was, Jesus replied:

> "The foremost is, 'Hear, O Israel: The Lord our God is one Lord;
> And you shall love the Lord your God with all your heart, and with all your soul, and with all your mind, and with all your strength.'
> "The second is this, 'You shall love your neighbor as yourself.'
> There is no other commandment greater than these" (Mark 12: 29-31).

The first commandment was already known. But the second one was uttered by Jesus for the first time.

FORGIVENESS OF OTHERS TO HEAL BODY, MIND, AND HEART

It was a few years back that I was watching the News on the television, and there was the report of a man who had abducted, and later killed, a five-year old Amish girl—somewhere in Pennsylvania, I believe. After this man was apprehended by the authorities, the parents of the little girl were interviewed, and they said that despite the tragedy that had occurred, they forgave the man for what he had done. He was obviously prosecuted and faced the full force of justice, but I was amazed at how unequivocal this Amish family was in their belief and practice of forgiveness. I was sitting on the couch thinking to myself that I doubted I could ever have forgiven anyone (or at least that quickly) had I personally been affected. But this is precisely what Jesus demanded of us. We must forgive so that we too can be forgiven, and saved.

Look at it from the point of view of your health once again. Unforgiveness entails us bottling up a host of harmful memories and emotions, that whenever we're reminded of the trauma that caused the resentment in the first place, we're literally tearing open the soul wound once again. That old pain doesn't seem to diminish, does it? We can feel that emotional upset all over again, as well as experience physical discomfort. Remember those harmful molecules our body makes when we possess a negative mindset? So in forgiving others, we break the chain of suffering that links us to them and to the event that triggered the trauma in the first place.

FORGIVENESS OF SELF

The past decade of wars in Iraq and Afghanistan have reminded us once again of not only the physical damage done to civilians, and soldiers on the frontlines of battle, but also the emotional and spiritual suffering they and their loved ones have to face.

Even though I've never been in a war, I am deeply grieved when I hear of cases of people suffering from Post-Traumatic Stress Disorder (PTSD), because I know that they are dealing with an unresolved trauma and unforgiveness at a level that no MRI or X-Ray machine can detect. And this on top of the stigma of mental illness these men and women have to cope with.

I've seen heartbreaking documentaries of soldiers who have been receiving treatment for this disease, and on more than one occasion I saw relief come across their faces when they said that the biggest obstacle they had to deal with, and had eventually conquered, was survivor guilt. They were living with the terrible guilt of having seen their comrades killed in front of them, but they were the privileged ones to have lived. In the end, they said they had learned it was okay to have survived, and they could stop punishing themselves and genuinely forgive themselves. A huge burden was lifted, which opened a path for further healing. So we must also remember to forgive ourselves, because most times in life, we are our own worst critics.

Although not as significant as suffering from PTSD, I dealt with an early case of childhood guilt that took years to get over.

When I was in the second grade, I was bullied by a kid who was a year older than me. He would trip me and throw me to the ground at every opportunity during recess time, all the while he had a bigger sidekick who would simply laugh in delight every time, but never actually do anything to me. I figured my oppressor was jealous because he had to wear thick pop-bottle glasses, and I didn't. In fact, he would call *me* "four eyes" every time he finished knocking me down.

After about the third time of this, I remember praying on my knees at my bed for God to kill this kid for me. I had never prayed in my life before, and had no idea what else to do. I was totally embarrassed about crying to my teacher or parents about the guy. Besides, I figured my father would beat me silly for not fighting back.

Well, I bravely walked to school the next day quite sure I would be beat up during the first recess period, as usual. Morning recess came and went, and I didn't see "Darth Vader" and "Grand Moff Tarkin" (the movie, *Star Wars* was big at the time) anywhere. I also didn't see them outside after lunch, or for the last recess period of the afternoon. *Strange*, I thought, *but good.*

So the next day came, and as soon as we had heard the national anthem and prayed the Lord's Prayer that were broadcast over the school intercom, our teacher told us that there was some bad news she had to tell us—a student had died in a car accident the day before, and that we'd be joining up with the grade three class the boy was in (right next door to us) to collectively pray for his soul. I had a strange feeling in my belly.

As we were walking over, some of the little gossip girls began saying who it was, and it was *my* bully! I was in a state of shock, but fortunately we didn't have far to go, and we all sat down while our teachers began to lead us in prayer.

I was strangely elated, but also freaked out. I thought it was *my* fault that "Vader" had died. I looked up, and in a solemn reflection knew there was "Someone upstairs who had my back."

When I got home from school, I pulled open the *London Free Press* newspaper to see the article about the accident, and there it was, a photo of his face, glasses and all. I felt so guilty and sick to my stomach. It took me years to get over the feeling, and only by realizing that I wasn't responsible for what had happened. I finally forgave myself.

As for the bully's sidekick, I would see him wandering alone in the playground from time to time. Once, he stopped and sheepishly looked at me, then quickly walked away. I don't think that poor kid was ever the same. Later on, I got a better sense of the impact we can suffer beneath the skin.

In the late 1990s when I was an auxiliary police constable with the London Police Service, I attended three suicide scenes in my first week of uniformed patrol service. And for that, I was baptized with the nickname of "Auxiliary of Death." I was so embarrassed, and had to repeatedly tell my fellow auxiliaries that my experiences were *not* "cool," and that I *wasn't* lucky to have gotten "all the action." One of the calls in particular, prevented me from sleeping for a week, and I couldn't get the person's face out of my head. I was likely suffering from a mild case of post-traumatic stress, but this diagnostic label hadn't been popularized yet.

Constable "Davids" and I were called to look into a report of a missing older male. When we arrived at the house, we met the man's wife, and his stepdaughter, who ended up doing all the talking, while her mother remained stone silent. We got the whole story from her, but she seemed quite nervous when she explained that her stepfather had gone for a ride on his bicycle and hadn't been home for a couple of days, which of course, was not like him. The usual places he'd hang around had said they hadn't seen him either.

While we were looking around the house, I asked her where else "Moe" might be keeping information that could lead us to his whereabouts. She paused for a few moments, looked at Davids, then at me, and murmured, "The garage." Davids and I glanced at each other and we ran outside to the detached garage. He nudged the side door open a bit, and there was the unfortunate little man, hanging from one of the ceiling beams from a rope that had been strung around his neck. The scene was surreal, and my mind tried to trick me into believing it was just a mannequin, that it wasn't really a person hanging there with a very long neck, no complexion, and green mucus hanging down from his chin.

Davids pulled out his pocket knife and said, "Okay, hold him while I cut him down."

I froze, and was going to protest, but knew that would be pointless; I was the auxiliary, and I didn't have a pocket knife.

I had a hard time comprehending what would drive someone to take their own life, but now I understand that a deep enough heart wound, and separation from hope, can lead to someone giving up. One thing I'll never forget, was seeing a beautiful painting of Jesus Christ hanging in the man's bedroom, prior to us figuring out he was in the garage. And yes, I was perplexed as to the meaning of the image of Christ.

For some, religious iconography is used for decoration, but for others, it defines their faith.

So how do we go about explaining childhood illnesses? After all, how could the average one-year old be holding a grudge against anyone? I can say that in these cases, it is nothing the child has done. Our love, our prayers, and medical science are the only things we can do to overcome childhood disease.

UNTYING THE KNOTS OF OLD HABITS

Jesus' ultimate act of forgiveness was when He was dying on the cross, and He uttered:

> "Father forgive them; for they do not know what they are doing" (Luke 23:34).

Jesus placed everyone else ahead of His own pain and suffering. And this after the horrible abuse He received. He was mocked, punched, spat on, had part of His beard torn out, had a crown of thorns jammed into His head, and was scourged until His flesh was ripped. He then had to carry His own heavy wooden cross to the place of His execution, and then was nailed to it. Truly, had His persecutors known the consequences of their actions, they would have refrained from doing them. And so, if Jesus Himself was able to forgive, how then can we ever not forgive anyone who has harmed us?

You might be asking, "Okay, we should forgive, but should we not set a limit? That is, is it right to just keep on forgiving? That just means people can keep on ruining other people's lives without any consequences."

There are in fact consequences to all bad behavior. Forgiving someone does not mean they are off the hook. They do need to be made aware of their actions, and do need to face justice if they've committed a criminal act. And from the standpoint of the spiritual damage that may have been inflicted, they are still accountable to God.

Forgiving those who have trespassed against us means that we have released them from doing any further harm to our soul—we have released them, and ourselves, from that spiritual millstone that has been hanging around our neck. This allows us to move on with our lives rather than to be continually looking back with regret or depression.

And do you know what? Nowhere is it written that once you've forgiven someone you are obligated to still hang around them, especially if you don't live or work with them. We still need to be wise, and distance ourselves from those who don't add value to our wellbeing.

How ready are you to do some serious internal cleansing? I did the following exercise several months ago, and in fact, have been doing it ever since, and I'm still surprised at all of the baggage that keeps coming up. It has left me in awe of how vast, and essentially limitless, is the mansion of our soul.

Just a word of caution: If you plan on mimicking what I did, you may want to start off slow here, and leave the tougher cases until you're ready to confront them. We all know the most significant cases of people who have mistreated us. Thoughts of them may come to mind regularly, or once in a blue moon. Perhaps you've already forgiven them, or at least you "think" that you have. Over time, you should begin to feel lighter and more energized, and you just might notice that you have a higher opinion of people in general. But please, if you have any concerns about confronting the issues of your heart, or you are seeing a medical professional, have a heart-to-heart talk with them in advance, as your wellbeing should be part of a collective team approach.

Here is what I did. I went to my prayer room and began praying for Jesus to open my heart so that I could genuinely forgive and release everyone in my life who I thought had caused me grief in some way, no matter how trivial the transgression.

When images and faces came to mind, they arrived with varying degrees of thoughts and feelings like, *Jerk! Back stabber!* Or of me experiencing an ache in my chest. I was surprised, because I was taken right back to those instantaneous moments when the memory was formed, and that I had in fact not truly forgiven. I was still holding a grudge. When I focused more on the person and the feelings they elicited in my heart, I would then say, "I forgive you, and I release you. Be at peace."

For some it was easier than others. There was, however, one individual I had worked with years ago who had really gotten under my skin, and who had annoyed the heck out of me, that required at least ten prayer sessions to release. Yes, just like having performed the Rite of Exorcism on myself to drive out the demon. I thought I was never going to end up forgiving him. But persistence paid off. Like anything worthwhile, we need to apply sustained effort and keep working until we reach the finish line.

Forgiving someone, to me, is like draining a fatal venom, or poison, from your body, because I sincerely believe that if we fill ourselves up to the emotional brim with the toxicity of unforgiveness, it can kill us.

If forgiveness could have been measured like water, I'm sure I could have filled up several Olympic-size swimming pools. Honestly, when I started off, I thought I'd have to deal with as many people as I could count on my fingers (and maybe toes), but then more and more "ghosts from the past" kept showing up! Some things I thought I had completely forgotten about because I had assumed they were insignificant, but the soul doesn't forget anything—it is like a video recorder that keeps on recording. Even now, the odd thing comes up from the depths of time, and I release the person and event with sincerity as soon as I can.

I try not to get into all the minute details of what was said and what was done. Rather, I let the feelings in my heart find their own balance, and I let the person and event as whole, go.

In the end, the greatest concern we need to have in our existence is the state of our soul. After all is said and done, it's all we've got. It is known, and should be of no surprise, that one of the biggest concerns a dying person has is to be forgiven by those people they betrayed or harmed. It's like the soul's wisdom completely overrides the egoic mind and reminds us of what truly matters—our relationships.

About a decade ago when my maternal grandfather had been visiting us from Europe, he sensed he would never see me again, and as we were saying our goodbyes, he profusely asked that I forgive him for anything he may have said or done that may have offended me. I really couldn't think of anything because he was quite an honest and upright individual, and I thought his request was really not required, and in fact, overdramatic. I naturally said, "Of course, Grandpa, but you haven't offended me in any way." It wasn't long afterward that he passed away.

But now I understand the significance of his request. He needed to be clear in his own conscience, and not carry any doubt or guilt that he had forgotten about anything.

I think it is too easy for us to sweep events under the carpet and mutter that God won't care or hold certain small things against us. But I'm of the mind that on Judgment Day, when we stand before the Lord Jesus, our soul will be reflected back to us like in a mirror. We shall see and experience every single moment of our lives, and we will, in a way, be judging our actions just as Jesus will be judging us. We will know whether or not we have truly let go of all our selfish grudges:

> "For if you forgive men for their transgressions, your heavenly Father will also forgive you. But if you do not forgive men, then your Father will not forgive your transgressions" (Matthew 6: 14-15).

BLESSING OTHERS

Now we need to take our potential for healing one step further. We need to bless the people that we have forgiven. At this point you're saying, "You've got to be kidding me! After I've forgiven that person, now I should bless them with health, wealth, and happiness? Let them find their own!"

My reply to this is to stop being selfish. Stop being like the older son of the parable of the prodigal son who was jealous when his father took back his younger brother after he had squandered his inheritance in frivolous living away from home (see Luke 15: 11-32). Again, Jesus said this:

> "But I say to you, love your enemies, and pray for
> those who persecute you[.]" (Matthew 5: 44).

I know for me, that when I forgive someone, and then bless them, I completely prevent myself from ever having a negative opinion about that person ever again. It's like wrapping a present with forgiveness and placing the bow of blessing on top. It completes the gift. Indeed, you're not only giving your "brother" or "sister" this gift, but to yourself as well. So your prayer could go something like this:

> *Lord Jesus, from the depths of my soul, I forgive and release this person, and I also bless them with joy, success, and happiness.*

Once you have this routine as part of your daily life, you just might start to notice things change about those same people you still interact with. As your perception shifts, they will assuredly begin to change their behavior towards you. When you send out the best of your heart, you will receive it in kind:

> "For whatever means you deal out *to others*, it will be
> dealt to you in return" (Luke 6: 38).

31

CHAPTER THREE

Faith in Christ

"Jesus answered and said to them, "This is the work of God, that you believe in Him whom He has sent" (John 6: 29).

"DJ Gabe Wolff," a Polish-Ukrainian friend of mine (who looked remarkably like the fashion model, Fabio) from my days at Sir Wilfrid Laurier high school, owned a downtown night club called, "Atomic Pulsar," where he played various genres of music. Most nights it was retro synth-pop from the 1980s, such as *Duran Duran, a-ha, The Human League*, and other bands I was vaguely familiar with. But Fridays and Saturdays he catered to the "goth" crowd—a mix of tattoo-covered young adults and older professionals, such as doctors, lawyers, and accountants, who painted their faces white, put on black eyeliner and lipstick, dyed their hair black, and wore black leather and various other sado-masochistic garments.

The first goth night I attended, I swore I was in the opening scene of the movie, *Blade*, starring Wesley Snipes as the day-walking vampire slayer, where the partier found himself surrounded by a crush of blood-ravenous vampires. The only thing missing was the blood raining down from the ceiling sprinklers. The lyrics and beat were very dark and heavy electro music by the band, *Combichrist*. I was so clean cut and out of place that I felt like Richie Cunningham from the TV show, *Happy Days*, at a Rob Zombie concert.

I didn't have a place to hang out on weekends at the time, so I decided to see what my friend's place was all about. One thing I never did was judge anyone there—I always treated them with respect—in spite of their Halloween outfits—because I felt that if I didn't like them, then I also had no business being there. I also rationalized that even Jesus spent time among sinners, and the lost.

I came to know many of the patrons quite well and was amazed at their intellectual and social-revolutionary acuity. They were definitely fringe society, but were proud of it.

I had quite a few engaging discussions on politics with a real burly and rough-looking biker type, who called himself, "Falcon." He sported a beard and moustache, had long black hair past his shoulders, tattoos covering both his arms—he never wore long sleeves—only a worn and cracked black leather vest to complement his torn jeans and Doc Martens. He was a self-proclaimed alcoholic and drug user, but deep inside, I could tell that he was a good person, one who was trying to find himself.

A month after I had come to know him, I no longer saw Falcon for quite some time, so I asked one of his little toadie friends, "Hey, where's Falcon been? I haven't seen him around for a while."

He looked up at me with glazed eyes and said in a raspy voice, "Oh dude, I've got really bad news. Falcon's dead."

I was caught off guard. "What?! How did it happen?

He took a long sip of his rye and coke, then replied, "He was being chased by some drug dealers on some building rooftops when they shot him and then he fell three stories into a garbage dumpster, dead." He then walked away and joined up with a few of his friends at the bar. *Hmmm . . . guess Falcon didn't fly to safety that night*, I sadly thought.

About three months passed, and while I was talking with Gabe at the DJ booth, I saw what I thought could only be a ghost—or a doppelganger—walk into the club. It was Falcon! I called to him, and he walked over to me.

"Falcon, one of your buddies told me you were killed, that you'd been shot and left for dead in a dumpster!"

"Yeah, that's the official story. But what happened was that when I was shot at—oh man, something came over me—I called out to Jesus to save me." He paused solemnly, and then continued. "As I was being shot at, I jumped off the roof, landed in the dumpster, and played dead until they went away laughing at how they had wiped me out."

He then pulled back his vest and showed me the new tattoo he had engraved on the left side of his chest. It was a large cross, and in the middle of it was the head of Jesus with a crown of thorns. "See this? The Lord rescued me. I didn't even get a bruise that night. I'm through with drugs, forever."

I was speechless. Psalm 91 (verses 11-12) immediately came to mind:

> "For He will give His angels charge concerning
> you,
> To guard you in all your ways.
> They will bear you up in their hands,
> Lest you strike your foot against a stone."

I reflected that we never know under what circumstances we'll find our faith in Christ.

Jesus' ministry showed us that illness is part of being human, but that through faith, we can overcome *any condition*. For it is faith that we have been operating through in the previous discussion of prayer, forgiveness, and blessing. We can't see the forces at work, but we know what their results are—our healing.

How do I define faith? Faith is like when you put one foot in front of the other when you are walking. Do you doubt that you'll take the next step, or are you *certain* you will? Faith is like that. We have an awareness that no proof is needed, because we possess the inward experience and knowledge that something is true and reliable. Again, faith entails the absence of any doubt.

Where there is doubt, we lack the confidence to see something through to completion. Just think of when you may have been driving in an unknown city, and you weren't sure if you were driving east or west. Compare that to the town you live in. You drive to and from home without even thinking about it, because there is no doubt or confusion.

Faith defeats the scoffer and moves mountains. It works hand-in-hand with our imagination, because it is not bound by limitations. It doesn't worry about the opinions of unbelievers who tell you, "That can't be done," or "You don't have the ability to fulfill your dreams."

Faith does not require proof, because proof functions at the level of the egoic mind, the false self; whereas faith resides at the level of your heart, your soul. And how exactly can one weigh or measure the soul?

I've often been asked why people who are ill don't get better even after all the prayers they have received. I don't know God's plans for an individual's life, but I can only say that in some cases, it is our own lack of faith that prevents us from being cured. We have to open up our heart to allow the healing in—I don't believe it can forced upon us. I'd compare this to calling someone who doesn't answer their phone. You can't communicate unless that person decides to accept your call. When Jesus calls, do you answer?

Over and over again, the accounts of Jesus performing miraculous healing show how the faith of the afflicted made them well, and how they sought Jesus out so they could be restored. Faith motivated and drove them to touch and ask Jesus to impart His power upon them; their actions serve as an example for all of us to follow:

> "And behold, a woman who had been suffering from
> a hemorrhage for twelve years, came up behind
> Him and touched the fringe of His cloak; for she
> was saying to herself, "If I only touch His garment,
> I shall get well."
>
> But Jesus turning and seeing her said, "Daughter,
> take courage; your faith has made you well." And
> at once the woman was made well" (Matthew 9:
> 20-22).

When we pray to Jesus to be liberated of our burdens, we
are to be driven and motivated by our conviction and faith
in Him. And we know that where faith is absent, little, to
nothing, is accomplished. This is no more evident than when
Jesus was largely rejected by His own people of Nazareth, the
village where He was raised:

> "And when the Sabbath had come, He began to
> teach in the synagogue; and the many listeners were
> astonished, saying, "Where did this man *get* these
> things, and what is *this* wisdom given to Him, and
> such miracles as these performed by His hands?
>
> "Is not this the carpenter, the son of Mary, and
> brother of James, and Joses, and Judas, and Simon?
> Are not His sisters here with us?" and they took
> offense at Him.
>
> And Jesus said to them, "A prophet is not
> without honor except in his home town and among
> his *own* relatives and in his *own* household."
>
> And He could do no miracle there except that
> He laid His hands upon a few sick people and
> healed them.
>
> And He wondered at their unbelief" (Mark 6:
> 2-5).

CONFIDENCE

I've witnessed how the undoing of emotional blockages can liberate a person from pain and suffering, usually from unknown biological causes.

A while back, "Roger," a co-worker, and friend of mine, had begun to complain about muscle and nerve pain in his right hand, and running up the length of his arm to his shoulder. He said he hadn't been doing anything different in terms of his exercise routine, or when he slept at night. The pain, however, prevented him from using his right hand most of the day, and he experienced difficulty sleeping. He then began seeing a Traditional Chinese Medical Doctor for acupuncture treatment.

When Roger told me this, the movie, *My Life*, starring Michael Keaton, came to mind, and the feeling crossed me that my friend was probably suffering from something emotional that was displaying as physical pain.

Our body and soul are united, so one will always impact the other. In my experience, the body will end up storing unresolved emotions somewhere in the body, which then begin to affect our mood and energy levels.

The next day, I was talking with a female co-worker, and she said, "Oh, did you know that Roger is going to start his new role next week because he got promoted?"

I replied, "No, I didn't know, but that's great." Now I knew that this position was a big step for anyone, let alone him, and there was a lot of stress for those initially starting out.

After several sessions of having needles stuck into him, I asked Roger how he felt. He said he "seemed" to be getting better, but that he had stopped seeing the acupuncturist because he wasn't able to isolate the nerves that were causing him so much grief.

I then asked him how he felt about the new role he was starting the following week, and he stared at me for a moment, and then said he was really looking forward to it. I reassured him that he would be having a lot thrown at him, but that in my position as the department's Process and Training Coordinator, and friend, I'd provide him with all the mentoring and support that he needed to succeed, and that if he had any self-doubt, to put it all aside, because everyone else on the team would also be there to back him up. He appreciated that, and as he left, I silently prayed for the full restoration of his physical health, and his confidence.

The next day when I went down the hall to his office and asked how everything was, he said he felt pretty good, and that the pain seemed to have completely vanished. Roger was once again using his right hand on the computer keyboard. Although others may not know who Jesus is, we can pass our confidence and trust that we have in Him on to them.

Nearly two years ago when I went back to Ontario to spend time with my family for the Christmas holidays, it happened that a dear family friend of ours was in the hospital suffering from stomach cancer. My paternal grandfather had died of this same disease, so we knew how bad the pain was. No one was saying her condition was terminal, but in my gut, I sensed she wouldn't live past Christmas. And so it was that we got the sad phone call from her husband during the afternoon of Christmas Day telling us that she had passed away.

Days leading up to her friend's death, my mother was very upset, and was gravely saddened for her condition. Not only did her heart ache, but she began having unexplained abdominal pain. She asked if I could help, and I said, "Of course," because I knew her condition was emotional.

After praying at the pain, and discussing the nature of the emotions that she felt when she placed her awareness to her belly, she realized she was bottling up her own fear of death, and the helplessness of not being able to help our dying friend. I reminded my mother that our faith in Jesus of Nazareth gave us hope that death is not the end; that we would all see each other again when He returns and we are resurrected to eternal life. She then began to spontaneously feel better, and she said the ache in her heart subsided, followed by the pain in her abdomen. And every so often, she reminds me how I had healed her, and that she is still pain free. I have to laugh and continually correct her that *Jesus* healed her because of her confidence in Him. I was merely the "tour guide" who brought her to that place of realization.

I don't recall where I read this, but the author said something like this, "Intent is more engulfing than reason. Intent can go through walls." *A page right out of the Gospels*, I thought.

Where would any new discovery or breakthrough in any field of human endeavor have gone had we not acted at a level of faith? Easy—we would not have gotten anywhere. Why then do we put barriers up before ourselves, thinking health and prosperity are limited to a select and lucky percentage of the overall population? Somehow, I don't recall Jesus making class or background distinctions. Our ability to reach our unlimited potential is universal.

If we don't have a pre-existing pattern of success, it is easy for us to fall into our old habits of doubt and fear that we'll be criticized and laughed at by others for pursuing our dreams. Don't worry about them; have faith and keep your focus on Jesus. Focus on your target and don't let the distracting self-defeating chatter of your egoic mind break your attention. Jesus reminds us that it doesn't even take that much faith or trust to achieve greatness:

> "And the Lord said, "If you had faith like a mustard seed, you would say to this mulberry tree, 'Be uprooted and be planted in the sea'; and it would obey you" (Luke 17:6).

So in other words, what may appear to be impossible, is possible with faith. But without any, we can do nothing.

The more you live in trust, the more it will increase in size and depth. What once were insurmountable obstacles will begin to be more manageable, because your faith is a reassurance of the partnership you have established with Jesus to work through all of the trials and difficulties that may appear in life. You will be assured that you're not fighting the battle alone, that you will overcome and succeed. And there's no one out there who can tell you otherwise. Case in point is the countless number of people who are told by their doctors that they have a terminal illness, and that they have only a few months, or weeks, to live.

When that patient, and those that care about them, turn to their faith in Christ, and "miraculously" defeat their prognosis, then we know therein lies the proof of the supernatural hand of God, His Son, and the Holy Spirit at work in the world.

"Okay, so I've got faith," you say. But did you know it needs to be maintained and cultivated, that it can grow stronger, or can be lost? It isn't something we just get once and put in our wallets and then forget about.

Faith grows stronger with our use of it. The more you pray and conduct your life in a state of complete trust in Christ, you will be boosting your faith every time. And as Jesus said, you will get more of it:

> "Therefore take care how you listen; for whoever has, to him shall *more* be given; and whoever does not have, even what he thinks he has shall be taken away from him" (Luke 8: 18).

But faith can be a tricky thing, because our egoic mind is always with us until the day we die. In part, its job is to keep the body safe from harm, such as in the fight-or-flight response, when our adrenal glands begin pumping out stress hormones for when we either have to fight, or run away, from trouble. It prompts us to get up in the morning so we can earn money to put bread on the table. In all, it ensures our material needs are accounted for.

Some would refer to the egoic mind, however, as "the devil." I don't entirely agree. The devil, and ignorance, can certainly use it as an opening into us in order to sidetrack us, but as long as we keep it in check, and let it know who is boss, then we can move forward without looking over our shoulder all of the time.

I'm like anyone else, and every so often, this little tiny bit of doubt of the deity of Jesus Christ creeps into my mind like, *Will He really come again to judge the living and the dead?* Or, *What if His miracles weren't real, but only fairy tales?* But I quickly understand that this is my rational mind at work, for deep in my heart I already possess the personal knowledge of the truth of who He is.

Such doubts, when they wander in, are as the stumbling blocks that Jesus told us are inevitable, and for us to be watchful of. His advice to us is to have authority over negative thoughts—to "rebuke"them, or in essence, tell them to go "jump in the lake." Even His disciple, Simon Peter, felt the blunt end of one of Jesus' rebukes when he was trying to dissuade Jesus from going to Jerusalem, where He would be seized and put to death. Jesus said,

> "Get behind Me, Satan! You are a stumbling block
> to Me; for you are not setting your mind on God's
> interests, but man's" (Matthew 16:23).

You can certainly use the "Get behind me, Satan" verse to rid your mind of doubt. I myself choose to engage negativity with this short, yet effective, prayer:

> *Lord Jesus, by my acknowledgment that You have*
> *overcome the world, and by Your stripes (suffering), no*
> *more fear, worry, anxiety, doubt, or stress exist in me*
> *anymore. They are finished forever. Amen.*

It is easy to see that even in His own company of friends Jesus had to be on guard against being pushed off course. And so, we too must be aware of the company we keep, and how they affect us. For those family and friends who truly care about us, we would be wise to be direct and polite with them when they engage in opinions and criticism of us that may knowingly, or unknowingly, cause us to doubt the path we are on. Calling them "Satan," and telling them to get behind us, may not be ideal (you can certainly say this in your head), but a sincere word from the heart is just as effective. And once we've made our decision, we must be resolute, and continually listen to our heart, until our desire has been fulfilled.

I'm always at a loss for words when I'm reminded of Jesus fixing His mind to go to Jerusalem, even though He knew He would be tortured and killed. If He had the unbending intent to carry out His mission, how much easier then is it for us to pursue that which *won't* kill us, but rather bring us joy?

The disowned part of ourselves, or our "shadow," as I refer to it, is a dimension of our soul that has been wounded, and which we are afraid to confront. Jesus allows us to look directly at this pain so we can let the burden go.

Have you ever known a man and woman who initially hated one another and then, for whatever reason, broke down and fell madly in love with each other? Our shadow works something like this. The things that disgust us about another person (so long as they are not criminal or immoral in nature) may just be aspects of ourselves that we are afraid to look at. We can never fully heal if we fight, or run away from, that "ugly" part of ourselves. We need to gently examine it and engage it. And when we embrace our shadow, we can fully love ourselves, and others.

United States President Franklin D. Roosevelt told the American people during the Great Depression of the 1930s that the only thing they had to fear was fear itself. Fear is that great weapon that Satan uses to confuse us and drain us of our confidence.

When doubt and fear emerge, remember to always invoke the name of Jesus for renewed confidence, because He overcame all the worry in this world. Also, you can use this opportunity to not only break an old, limiting behavior, but to change the relationship you have with yourself because that aspect of yourself that you're keeping locked away could end up being a source of strength and knowledge for you.

Back when I was in a senior mathematics course in high school, "Jake," a friend of mine who sat behind me in class, always got agitated about learning new concepts, and even more so when it came to writing tests or examinations (but, then again, don't most of us?).

One day, I turned around in my seat, looked at him, and told him, "You know, you can never learn and master something if you fear it."

He was very appreciative of the advice, and said he had never thought of it that way. He then began to approach learning as his *friend*, rather than his enemy. Jake engaged that disowned part of himself—his shadow—and he appeared more confident thereafter.

CHAPTER FOUR

The Law and Prosperity

"I tell you, there is joy in the presence of the angels
of God over one sinner who repents" (Luke 15:10).

That week, I decided not to pay for parking on campus
while I was taking an afternoon business course up at
Western (the University of Western Ontario). I didn't have a
parking pass—I used the pay meters, putting in the necessary
king's ransom of coins into the machines so I wouldn't get a
hefty fine.

Not only had I decided to skip paying for parking, I chose
a stall that was reserved for professors, right beside one of the
university buildings that I had observed was always vacant, and
was a minute's walk to my class, and thus, very convenient. Call
it arrogance, call it hubris—I was out to flaunt it to the law of
the almighty university system, just because I wanted to.

Day one—Monday—I left class, and there was my 1987
Honda Accord glimmering in the afternoon sun, with not so
much as a parking ticket on the windshield. *Excellent*, I thought.
*I guess the meter maids assume I'm the professor who owns the
privilege of this spot—why else would anyone park here?*

Tuesday gave me the same gift of ease and savings. Wednesday and Thursday were also fine free. I gloated how my shrewd business acumen was paying dividends.

I guess I hadn't paid attention to the weather forecast on Friday, because I was surprised when it began raining as I drove onto campus. I didn't have a rain jacket, but thankfully, I didn't have to worry about it because I could just sprint to the business building, due to its proximity.

As I left class, it was really raining cats and dogs. I ran to my car but got completely soaked by the time I flung the car door open and dove in. As I turned on the ignition, I saw that dreaded piece of paper. The parking ticket was pinned beneath the left windshield wiper blade, and it was plastered to the glass as it was just as drenched as I was.

What the . . . How dare they give me a ticket! What kind of a moronic idiot goes around writing up parking fines in the rain! I was flabbergasted, and felt that I had been unfairly treated, or rather, unfairly caught.

I carefully removed the sopping wet paper, looked at the penalty, and threw it onto the passenger seat. It was heftier than usual because I had been parked in a reserved area. And it wasn't reserved for me.

As I drove home, with the injustice of my treatment foremost in my mind, the weather began to clear up. But as luck would have it, I was pulled over by the police because I was speeding above the posted limit. I didn't even say a word when the officer handed me the ticket; I simply tossed it on top of the one I had just gotten ten minutes earlier.

At this point, I wasn't angry, because I was too busy reasoning that there must be some conspiracy at work here—if not human, then the forces of the universe were working against me. I felt like a gambler who had pushed his luck one too many times and had lost his winnings to the house—the odds of probability had eventually beaten me.

"Well, thankfully I'm almost home and can put this punishing day behind me," I consoled myself, driving off. But my extra-curricular learning wasn't over yet.

Inexplicably, the engine began to lose power. I quickly pulled to the side of the road, and the car coasted until I braked and brought it to a stop. I turned on the ignition several times, but the car wouldn't start. It was like it had simply died.

I put both hands on the steering wheel, and said, "Okay. I get it, Lord. You've got my attention. I'm sorry. I don't know what got into me this week, but please forgive me. I will set my ways straight." I sat there for a while, feeling relieved, and at peace. It was like a load had been lifted from me.

I called the auto club, and a tow truck came to haul my Honda (and me) to the mechanic. Fortunately, it had only been the fuel pump that had died, and they replaced it quickly and affordably. I got home in time for supper.

LIVING BY THE COMMANDMENTS OF GOD FOR SUCCESS

If you haven't noticed already, when you not only go against your conscience, but established laws, be they those found in the Bible, ones made by people, or natural ones, such as the Law of Gravity, things don't usually work out all that well for you. You may think you've escaped from being noticed, and have "gotten ahead" by outsmarting people, but your inner environment is diminished. Neither will you escape from your deeds in your finite lifetime, nor on Judgment Day. Jesus cautioned us to always be "good fruit" in life, and to follow God's laws:

> "A good tree cannot produce bad fruit, nor can a rotten tree produce good fruit.
>
> Every tree that does not bear good fruit is cut down and thrown into the fire.
>
> So then, you will know them by their fruits.

Not every one who says to Me, 'Lord, Lord,'
will enter the kingdom of heaven; but he who does
the will of My Father who is in heaven" (Matthew
7:18-21).

Like the words that come out of our mouth that can defile
us, all of our good intentions and actions come from the heart.
And when we act out of fairness and concern for each other,
we contribute to everyone's wellbeing and success. The letter
of the law is important, but not more important than the spirit
of the law. When we know why rules exist, then we can respect
them better.

MONEY

"Beware, and be on your guard against every form of
greed; for not *even* when one has an abundance does
his life consist of his possessions" (Luke 12:15).

Greed is *not* a good thing if we set up money and objects as
gods that we worship. If we are pursuing wealth, then it must be
in repayment for the *good* we have provided to others—service
precedes the reward. Where people end up becoming lost
is when they have no faith in what Christ taught about our
relationship to "mammon," or material possessions. When
things go wrong, the unbeliever turns to science and other
men for all of their answers. So too, they measure their success
by comparing themselves to others. And when they fall short,
then they think that they are "losers," because somehow life is
a race that is based on the amount of goods you accumulate.
But this is exactly what Satan wants us to believe. He wants to
distract us and unplug us from our heart so that we spend all
of our time in the egoic mind. For it is here where we make our
comparisons and judgments of others, and of ourselves.

As for we Christians, we understand that earthly prosperity is a blessing, but does not last; that we are meant for an existence far beyond what we can see, smell, taste and touch. We are looking long-term, beyond the grave. In essence, we have far more to strive for in life—a prosperous one while we live in the here-and-now, *and* an eternal one.

It is telling when a man approached Jesus and asked how he could obtain eternal life:

> "He [Jesus] said to him,
> "One thing you still lack; sell all that you possess, and distribute it to the poor, and you shall have treasure in heaven; and come, follow me."
> But when he had heard these things, he became very sad; for he was extremely rich.
> And Jesus looked at him and said, "How hard it is for those who are wealthy to enter the kingdom of God!" (Luke 18: 22-24).

Jesus responded this way to the rich man as a challenge for him to shift his awareness as to what truly mattered in life. Even the thought of being separated from his possessions brought sadness to the man!

Store up wealth in your heart, because you can always go there to find your happiness and your peace. Think of the times you were loved, or how you enjoyed going to a particular vacation spot, or eating that chocolate sundae. Focus on the feelings, not on holding onto the stuff. When you can genuinely say to yourself that you are happy, because of how you feel, and not what you have, then you have begun to understand what Jesus meant by:

> "The kingdom of God is not coming with signs to be observed; nor will they say, 'Look, here *it is*! Or, 'There *it is*!' For behold, the kingdom of God is in your midst" (Luke 17: 20-21).

To me, being happy means being free of burdens, whatever form they may take—illness, guilt, debt, joblessness, and the million other things this world throws at us.

Jesus sought to remove the weight of judgment that was crushing us. He taught that we must place the word of the law upon our hearts, to adhere to the commandments at the level of feeling. For when we follow God's laws, we can set them as the foundation of our lives, and build upon them with confidence. These laws exist to maximize our happiness, and not as a form of control or punishment. For when we are commanded to "Not Commit Adultery," that is, to not cheat on our spouses or lovers, this is to protect everyone's wellbeing. And I don't need to get into an elaborate and lengthy discussion of how devastating it is when we discover that the one we love and trust has been intimate with someone else. This is one of the most destructive events that can befall a couple. Indeed, this can leave a very deep soul wound.

Cheating occurs first in our heart, and the damage is already done even if we don't actually approach and have intercourse with the person we're lusting for. For Jesus said it like this:

> "[B]ut I say to you, that every one who looks on a
> woman to lust for her has committed adultery with
> her already in his heart" (Matthew 5:28).

If we ignore God's laws—The Ten Commandments—the fame and wealth that we may have thought we earned through our *own* hard work and talents, may one day, all disappear. When I watch the news and see the ongoing scandals of movie stars, professional athletes, or politicians, I simply shake my head and ask myself, "Where was Jesus in their life? Where is their humility?" In worshipping their own image and having various extra-marital affairs, these societal role models end up selling their souls to the god of this world, and as a result, shake the love and trust of their family, friends, and admirers. And although they are "only human," and need our forgiveness when they fall from their heights of power and status, nevertheless, they do cause great harm to the wider world that looks up to them. Luke 12: 48 reminds us, that with prosperity, comes responsibility:

"And from everyone who has been given much shall much be required."

CHAPTER FIVE

Eternity

"For I have come down from heaven, not to do My own will, but the will of Him who sent me. And this is the will of Him who sent Me, that of all He has given Me I lose nothing, but raise it up on the last day" (John 6: 38-39).

S o you say, "Okay, fine. Jesus showed us that if we keep God's Commandments, and especially apply the "Golden Rule"—do unto others as you would have them do unto you—you can live a happy, stress-free life." But not only did Jesus come to show us the path to healing and abundance, He came to open the way to eternal life, an existence beyond the physical form we are familiar with.

Some Christians will no doubt disagree with some of my theological interpretations that are to follow, but I am staying true to what Jesus *Himself* taught, for He wanted us to be clear as to the promises He was making.

I don't know how many times I've heard this before, but countless believers rejoice over the belief that when they die, they will go straight to heaven, and be with loved ones forever. This is not what Jesus taught. Moreover, His death and resurrection would have had no value if this was the case. I'm not saying there isn't a heaven—it truly does exist, but we are not whisked away there at the moment of death (nor for that matter are evildoers plunged directly into the fires of hell). But just wait, and take courage for what I have to say.

Jesus adhered to His Jewish traditions and took them one step further. Judaism believed that the resurrection of the dead would occur at the end of time, on the "Last Day" (also known as Judgment Day, and the end of the age). Some Sadducees (a Jewish sect) asked Jesus about the nature of marriage at the time of the resurrection, and Jesus said to them,

> "The sons of this age marry and are given in marriage, but those who are considered worthy to attain to that age and the resurrection from the dead, neither marry, nor are given in marriage; for neither can they die any more, for they are like angels, and are sons of God, being sons of the resurrection" (Luke 20:34-36).

The story of the resurrection of Jesus' friend, Lazarus, also makes this point clear in the Gospel of John. This is what Jesus said to the grief-stricken Martha, the sister of Lazarus:

> "Your brother shall rise again."
> Martha said to Him, "I know that he will rise again in the resurrection on the last day."
> Jesus said to her, "I am the resurrection and the life; he who believes in Me shall live even if he dies, and everyone who lives and believes in Me shall never die" (John 11:23-26).

Jesus then raised Lazarus from "his sleep," from death. If he had gone to heaven, what then would it have profited Lazarus from being pulled out of eternal bliss, and put back in his body again? Surely, Jesus would have comforted everyone not to worry, because Lazarus was in a far better place. But this is *not* what happened.

Jesus impressed upon us that eternal life was not something frivolous and granted to everyone at the time of death. This gift came at a heavy cost, and Jesus had to pay the ransom with His own pain and death to set the captives of sin—all of us—free. Our sins, the breaking of God's divine laws by our actions and negative impulses of the heart, are those things which separate us from perfection. We are talking of spiritual separation here. Although we can't weigh the load of our sins, nevertheless, they are a very real burden that we all carry in this universe of energy and matter.

Jesus wanted us to be absolutely clear and confident in our understanding of the future that awaits us after we have passed away, or if we are alive when He returns. There is no communicating beyond the grave with the dead, there are no ghosts that consciously walk the earth haunting us, and there is no immediate flight to heaven when we die. The dead are dead—they are at rest in the earth until the day of His coming and judgment. As such, we are to live each day of our lives to the fullest, without regret or concern if someone is watching us from heaven, or hell, or someplace else that we may imagine. By throwing off all of the old wives' tales and New Age falsehoods of life after death, we can dedicate our attention to our hearts, and living fully in the present moment. For this is what Jesus wanted of us.

He said that everything in life is provided for us; even sin and death were conquered by Him. So our only job is to care for, and purify, our souls, and to follow God's laws, and love our neighbor. And thus, we can continually walk with one foot on earth, and the other in the kingdom of heaven. There is no mystery or magic behind this, only the truth of how you feel and share your love with others.

Jesus referred to death as "sleep" on several occasions. And this was no accident. He wanted to emphasize this relationship as a way for us to understand our own rising from death. If you were to wake up from a deep slumber, and if you didn't have a clock, or know what day it was, would you really know how much time had elapsed from the moment you closed your eyes to the moment you opened them? No.

Whether someone has been dead for one year, or a thousand years, each one of them will not sense that more time has passed for one over the other. In other words, the next conscious thought we'll have upon arising will be one of having been dead or "asleep," for just a fraction of a moment. We are promised that the next sight we'll see will be of Jesus Christ and a host of angels standing before us:

> "And then the sign of the Son of Man [Christ] will appear in the sky, and then all the tribes of the earth will mourn, and they will see the Son of Man on the clouds of the sky with power and great glory. And He will send forth His angels with a great trumpet and they will gather together His elect from the four winds [from the four corners of the globe], from one end of the sky to the other" (Matthew 24: 30-31).

And judgment of the living and the dead will follow:

> "For an hour is coming in which all who are in the tombs shall hear His voice, and shall come forth; those who did the good *deeds*, to a resurrection of life, those who committed the evil *deeds* to a resurrection of judgment" (John 5:28-29).

Again, Jesus wanted us to live a fruitful life, and not be distracted by illusions of communing with the dead. Hold your love and memories of those you have loved and known close to you always, and know that you will indeed see them again.

NEAR-DEATH EXPERIENCES

I am very familiar with the accounts and studies of Near-Death Experiences, or NDEs, such as in the work of Dr. Raymond Moody. And those who have either experienced them, or are die-hard believers of this phenomenon, will surely say, "Hey, people have gone to heaven and have seen grandparents, sons, daughters, and even pets they had, who had passed on. So this must be *proof* that people die and go to heaven, and that perhaps Jesus didn't explain life after death in enough detail."

Here is my take on this subject. Something this important would have been taught by Christ. And as I said earlier, this is contrary to all of what Jesus lived and died for. Yes, there appears to be a repetitive phenomenon at play here which goes generally like this: the individual has experienced some type of life-threatening trauma where they are either at the scene of the incident, or on a hospital bed; they die, or are dying; there is a rapid life review of every moment of their lives (like watching a movie in fast replay); then their consciousness lifts away from their body, and they are now hovering over, and looking down at it; they are then taken through a dark tunnel with a light at the end of it, and they are usually accompanied by angels or guides into the light; they enter a domain or dimension of light they had never experienced on earth. Some have said it showers them with love, and that there is an intelligence that "sees right through them." While in the light, multiple experiences occur. People see loved ones who have died, Jesus, and so on. Usually the recently deceased is asked what knowledge they have acquired, and how they have loved others. They are then told their time has not yet come to enter heaven, and that they must go back. And so they do, reluctantly, and regain consciousness in their bodies once again. For all, the experience is life-altering; they are never the same again.

There have also been accounts where people have experienced going to hell, and that by coming back to life, they were shaken to their core to become better people.

Our minds are very powerful and creative, and when we're at the point of death, they can muster strong survival and coping instincts. I believe that we can experience heaven in these instances, but that we do not go there permanently after death (of which, I will discuss further). As to the people the near-death experiencers see on the other side, I don't have an explanation, nor can I speak for those who are certain they interacted with individuals they knew. It could be that their consciousness generates them from their memories as a means of comforting their mind in light of the trauma they are experiencing.

The important thing to keep in mind is that near-death experiencers are changed on the inside, and live in renewed and increased faith. And this aspect of the event is a good thing.

ALL THE TIME IN THE UNIVERSE

So what will we do for all of eternity when Christ comes again? As Christ's resurrected form has demonstrated to us in the Gospels, we will enter the next phase of our journey where the boundaries of space and time will disappear. And just as we didn't know what we had in store for us when we were born into this world, neither will we know exactly in the next. But I'm guessing it will not be a dull existence. Many surprises await us in the kingdom of heaven.

You might be thinking, *Okay, so when Jesus returns, then if we pass the test of judgment, we'll go to heaven.* Well, no, not exactly. Even though heaven is the domain of God, and the source of our unlimited abundance, there will be a profound shift in the relation between heaven and earth at the end of days. This reality will fold into that of another; heaven and earth will merge to become one, and in the process, both will be transformed: "Heaven and earth will pass away, but My words will not pass away" (Luke 21: 33). And whenever I've mentioned the "kingdom of heaven," I was also describing the "kingdom of God," which refers to the *future kingdom* of heaven upon earth, when Christ comes again to rule as our King. Living each day in the kingdom of heaven is to live with our hearts in heaven *right now*, and in the future *expectation* of entering the kingdom of God.

You may ask, "But what about the thief on the cross that asked Jesus to remember him?":

> "Jesus, remember me when You come into Your kingdom!"
> And He said to him, "Truly I say to you, today you shall be with Me in paradise" (Luke 23: 42-43).

My interpretation of this is that Jesus did not mean the thief would go to paradise that day. Not at all, because Jesus Himself was going to descend into death, and then rise again on the third day—on the first day of the week (Sunday). And Jesus only ascended into heaven after appearing several times to his disciples in His glorified form.

I believe this statement is understood by repositioning the punctuation. The comma should go after the word, *today*. So what was meant was something like this, "Hey, let me tell you something right now ("today"). You have earned a future place in paradise with me because of your faith and repentance." And you will note that Jesus uses the term, "paradise," rather than "heaven." There is a distinction here, for He is referring to the *future* kingdom of heaven on earth, rather than heaven proper.

But what of other accounts of people going to, or being in heaven, such as the story of Lazarus and the rich man? Was not Jesus looking directly into heaven when He told this story?:

"Now there was a certain rich man, and he habitually dressed in purple and fine linen, gaily living in splendor every day.

And a certain poor man named Lazarus was laid at his gate, covered with sores, and longing to be fed with the *crumbs* which were falling from the rich man's table; besides, even the dogs were coming and licking his sores.

Now it came about that the poor man died and he was carried by the angels to Abraham's bosom; and the rich man also died and was buried.

And in Hades he lifted up his eyes, being in torment, and saw Abraham far away, and Lazarus in his bosom" (Luke 16: 19-23).

This account was a parable only, used to address the significance of our demeanor in life and how it would be accounted for at the end of the age when there would be a very clear awareness of the judgment we would be receiving. There shall be no middle ground—we will either find ourselves united with God, and dwell in the house of the Lord, forever (see Psalm 23), or separated from Him, for all eternity.

And whereas Jesus paid for our sins through His suffering, and the way was opened for us to enter into life everlasting, the rest is up to us. We can either use our God-given free will to love others, or we can choose to close ourselves off from our ultimate future by idolizing ourselves in this brief lifetime. Jesus' crucifixion was a very serious act for a very serious situation—our deliverance from darkness into light.

I knew a girl who abandoned her Catholic Church and took up New Age and Occult spirituality because of the contradictory and confusing answers she was receiving from her Catholic priests concerning heaven, and the resurrection.

Of one priest she had asked, "If when I die, will I be with my family in heaven?"

He said, "Yes."

Then she asked, "Why then will the dead be resurrected and judged upon Christ's Second Coming?"

He said, "That really isn't going to happen. We're judged as soon as we die, then we either go to heaven, or to hell." So in other words, "Jesus didn't know what He was talking about."

Finally, she asked, "Will I see my favorite pet dogs that I had as a child, in heaven, also?"

But the priest laughed and said, "Of course not, because heaven is only for people."

I think this last comment, above everything else, was what drove her completely out of Christianity. Ironically enough, Jesus did make reference to animals and their place in eternity:

> "Are not five sparrows sold for two cents? And *yet* not one of them is forgotten before God. Indeed, the very hairs of your head are all numbered. Do not fear, you are of more value than many sparrows" (Luke 12: 6-7).

Whenever in doubt, we need to go to the source of faith, which are the words and actions of our Master, and Teacher, Jesus of Nazareth. Therefore read the Gospels for yourself, and look for the very consistent direction given to us.

REINCARNATION

There are Christians who believe in Eastern and New Age concepts of reincarnation, or being reborn in a new body on earth. This is one of the pillars of Buddhism, in particular.

Buddhists believe that a person's deeds generate *karma* (which in Sanskrit means, "cause and effect"). Your good acts produce good karma, which translates into a better rebirth, while living an evil life will lead to a less favorable one. The goal is to purify your karma over successive lifetimes so that you will eventually break the cycle of suffering and confusion in this existence, known as Samara, and become enlightened, and in so doing, you will enter Nirvana, a state free of suffering, and thus never need to be reborn in an earthly form ever again.

I've been told before, that just because Jesus never taught about reincarnation, doesn't mean He didn't believe in it, or that it isn't real. Now in His day, there was some type of belief in reincarnation as in the following verses:

> "He began asking His disciples, saying, "Who do people say that the Son of Man is?"
>
> And they said, "Some say John the Baptist; some, Elijah; and others, Jeremiah, or one of the prophets."
>
> He said to them, "But who do you say that I am?"
>
> And then Simon Peter answered and said, "Thou are the Christ, the Son of the living God" (Matthew 16: 13-16).

But the concept of reincarnation was a myth believed in by the illiterate masses, for Judaism always professed that God gave man only one life to live:

> "Just as a man is destined to die once, and after that to face judgment . . ." (Hebrews 9:27).

Again, reincarnation is another delusion that Jesus did not want us wasting our time with. He upheld the tradition of His faith that we are each born in the image and likeness of God, and upon our resurrection, it will be the one and only *us*—not the "last bodily incarnation of a countless number of forms we've had since the beginning of the human race." This makes our conduct in the here-and-now even more imperative. There is no time to look back, only the immediacy of what we need to do to cultivate a good heart.

But some may ask, "What about the "scientific proof" of past lives, such as in the work of American psychiatrist, Dr. Brian L. Weiss?"

Several years ago when Dr. Weiss began performing regression therapy using hypnosis on some of his patients in order to tackle current issues that may have begun in early life, he began to notice that some of them would go "beyond" their childhood memories, and apparently into one or more previous incarnations they had had. And this after not having prompted or suggested that they do so. He, like the vast majority of the medical establishment, was a skeptic of the reality of past lives, but he began to see a re-occurring trend which he could not explain. In the end, he saw patients come to terms with events "of their past," which translated into healing of their present condition. Dr. Weiss has affirmed that he is not absolutely sure what is happening in the patient's mind, but the belief that they have healed an old wound is certainly something which has worked to restore them in the present.

I too can't get into the minds of those individuals who supposedly have past life memories, but I will once again say that the mind is a very powerful thing. And we certainly have not fully explored this great frontier. But, I do believe, as in the case of near-death experiences, that the mind can be creating a sense of structure to help comfort it, and bring balance to a situation it has been struggling to resolve. This may be a natural adaptive mechanism, and it does not mean that past lives are real.

IS KARMA THE SAME AS "WHAT YOU SOW IS WHAT YOU REAP"?

But didn't Jesus support the concept of karma? Not in the Buddhist way of thinking, He didn't. Buddhists do not believe in God or a Creator. Once again, Jesus followed and affirmed the tradition of Judaism, such as appears in Job 4:8: "As I have observed, those who plow evil and those who sow trouble reap it" (NIV). And in Luke 12: 24 which says, "Consider the ravens: they do not sow or reap, they have no storeroom or barn; yet God feeds them. And how much more valuable you are than birds!" In other words, our path in life is measured by God, and not in an impersonal, "karmic," mechanical way that allows gain or loss to occur across lifetimes—the matters of the heart and of sin are not defined by some universal mathematical equation that states, if you put "x" in, you get "y" out. The rewards or suffering of our actions occur in this life only—not in any future incarnation. And we shall be accountable for all of them on the day of judgment when Jesus returns to judge the living and the dead.

Once we begin to de-clutter our thoughts of all the superstition that the mass media have drowned us under, we can focus our energies on *this* life, the only one that has been gifted to us. And in placing Jesus at the head of our thoughts, we can walk with sharper awareness.

Before I was born again in Jesus Christ, I was heavy into the study of New Age spirituality, and particularly, Buddhism. Now I didn't shave my head, wear a saffron robe, or drink butter tea all day long, trying to experience the mysticism of being in a remote Tibetan monastery, but I did read everything I could get my hands on about it, and I meditated several times each day. I was very mindful of the Buddhist concept of karma, and especially how our acts from previous lifetimes could affect our present-day circumstances, or so this belief system proclaimed.

When I was the Land Administrator for an oil and gas exploration company based in Southern Ontario, I had, what I thought, was an experience of the real power of karma at work.

"Jennifer," the office accountant and receptionist, was a very energetic and friendly woman, and I had known her when I was an oil and gas leasing broker with another company I had worked for. So when I was hired on with her company,

I was very happy to be working with someone I had good relations with.

It wasn't all that long after, when I had fit into my new role, that the company President called me into his office and closed the door behind him, while directing me to sit down. I sensed something bad was afoot. He sat down in his big executive leather chair, behind his large wooden desk, and began telling me that Jennifer was the life of the company, and that if hell froze over, or the world came to an end, she would still be in his employ. He then said she was very upset with me regarding how I was treating her, that I talked down to her, and was disrespecting her. I couldn't believe what I was hearing. This was news to me since every time we talked, it was very casual, and we continually laughed at each other's jokes. I began to wonder what kind of lunacy I was dealing with here. My boss then concluded by saying, "If she complains to me again, I'll kick your arse across the 401" (a major highway that wasn't all that close to the office, but I still pictured him literally kicking my 187 centimetre, 83 kilogram frame up in the air, and over it like a punter would kick a football through the end zone uprights).

I absolutely had nothing I could say because I was in a state of shock. I put my head down and wandered back to my desk, and managed as best as I could to finish off the work day. Ironically, Jennifer hadn't come in to work that day—she had called in sick.

The next morning, I was the first to arrive at work, as usual, and a couple of hours into the morning, Jennifer still had not shown up. The company President walked in later in the morning, and he slowly approached my office, stood about an arm's length from me, and simply stared at me without saying a word. His eyes were protruding, and he didn't blink the whole time. And this lasted for several, uncomfortable, seconds. He then turned away and went to his own office. I thought to myself, *That was strange. I wonder what his problem is.*

A few minutes later, "George," the Vice President of Land, was called into the President's office, and I could hear them talking in a low tone. I couldn't make out what they were saying, but I could feel something unusual had happened.

George then walked over to see me and said that Jennifer was terribly ill and in the hospital, and that she was apparently paralyzed from the waist down.

I was once again, for the second straight day, in shock. It then dawned on me that, *This must be the infallible force of karma showing itself at work here.* Now you'd think that I'd be basking with satisfaction in light of the injustice that I had endured, but even I was surprised at my own reaction. I was neither sad, nor happy; I was completely unemotional about the whole thing. This didn't mean that I was heartless and didn't care, but I thought it was her destiny to go through this tragedy in order to discover deeper meaning in her life.

I was the first one from the company to go and visit her in the hospital the next evening. As I approached her room, I could see her lying down in bed on her side. I lightly knocked on the door jamb, saying her name. She opened her eyes, knew it was me, but couldn't get herself to look at me or even say anything. I sat down in the chair next to her bed, and I made small talk, about what, I couldn't remember now. It was very awkward.

A doctor came into the room to give her a brief examination. He tapped on various parts of her body with his index and middle finger, and as he was finishing, he had a slight, almost unnoticeable frown on his face, and glanced at me momentarily. The look he gave me pierced me, saying, "She'll never walk again." He then left.

After several more minutes of silence, I said goodbye to Jennifer, and she mumbled something I couldn't understand. I then left.

So what happened? Apparently, and this is only what I was told, was that Jennifer had been having acupuncture treatments, and she got blood poisoning from a needle that had been re-used, but improperly sterilized. The infection attacked her nervous system, resulting in paralysis, in addition to a few other complications. She became bound to a wheelchair, and she never ended up going back to work with us ever again.

It is only now, in reflective hindsight, that I know this event had nothing to do with bad karma, for Jennifer having done something harmful in a previous lifetime, or in this one. And it was neither an avenging angel unleashed by God to smite her down for what she had done to me. Ultimately, I don't know what God's plan was, but I do know that a profound shift in awareness occurred in everyone who knew her. It made us very mindful of the precious nature of life, and that we need to devote time to lifting each other up, rather than tearing one another down.

TRANSFIGURATION—THE "TEST DRIVE" OF THE INCORRUPTIBLE BODY

What we know we will look like at the resurrection of the dead was embodied by Jesus in both His transfiguration prior to His crucifixion, and when He rose from the dead and appeared to His friends. We have already seen the statement He made in Luke 20: 36, "for neither can they die any more, for they are like angels . . ." In other words, we shall possess spiritually transformed bodies different from the ones we currently have. These will be eternal, glorified bodies, where no illness, death, aging or heartache will ever again inhabit. We will have the ability to cross from spirit to form at will. We will, in essence, overcome Einstein's theory of relativity, and cut through the barriers separating distance, speed, and time. We will be able to dwell with one foot in the domain of spirit energy, while keeping the other one planted in material energy—the wind, earth, fire, and water—that we can physically feel. In the description of Christ's metamorphosis into a being of both form and light, we get our first glimpse of our future eternal bodies:

> "And six days later, Jesus took with Him Peter and James and John his brother, and brought them up to a high mountain by themselves.
>
> And He was transfigured before them; and His face shone like the sun, and His garments became as white as light" (Matthew 17: 1-2).

Our own resurrection will echo the transfiguration, in that we will discard our old selves like removing dirty, soiled clothing, and being dressed with fresh, bright garments. Think of it like seeing someone you know who dressed up for a ball, and you were utterly speechless at how incredible they looked, let alone barely recognizing them! And it is interesting to note that when Jesus had risen from the dead, His close friend, Mary of Magdalen didn't recognize Him when she was standing outside the empty tomb. She thought He was someone else, the gardener in fact:

> "She turned around, and beheld Jesus standing *there*, and did not know it was Jesus.
>
> Jesus said to her, "Woman, why are you weeping? Whom are you seeking?"
>
> Supposing Him to be the gardener, she said to Him, "Sir, if you have carried Him away, tell me where you have laid Him, and I will take Him away."
>
> Jesus said to her, "Mary!"
>
> She turned and said to Him in Hebrew, "Rabboni!" (which means, Teacher)" (John 20: 14-16).

What we also see is that we shall retain the form, personality, and memories of our former self. For although Christ now possessed a luminous, incorruptible (not subject to decay or dissolution), and immortal body, He was still essentially Himself.

But our passing beyond death will change our awareness. We will cease to perceive through the egoic mind, and instead, radiate our whole being through our true self—our heart—at a level that is completely unbounded by the former fears and confusion of the world that has passed away. And then we shall attain union with God and finally realize our infinite potential.

The resurrected Jesus was the prototype of our future ability to overcome the conventional barriers of reality. In His first resurrected appearance to His disciples who were in hiding, He passed through, and into, a sealed room:

> "When therefore it was evening, on that day, the first *day* of the week, and when the doors were shut where the disciples were, for fear of the Jews, Jesus came and stood in their midst, and said to them, "Peace be with you" (John 20:19).

And yet, He also took on a solid form in the Gospel of Luke:

> "See My hands and My feet, that it is I Myself; touch Me and see, for a spirit [or a "ghost"] does not have flesh and bones as you see that I have" (Luke 24: 39).

And:

> "He said to them, "Have you anything here to eat?"
> And they gave Him a piece of a broiled fish; and He took it and ate it in their sight" (Luke 24: 41-43).

Jesus meant to show us that He was not *just* a spirit, or immaterial in nature, but far more than that—substantial and complete. "Not conceivable," the skeptics may venture. But how much more miraculous is it to possess a glorified body that can shift "between heaven and earth" than it is for us to be born into the soul and body we have in the first place?

HEAVEN AND EARTH

Those who have lived an upright existence, and who are alive when Christ returns, will be transfigured into luminous beings, while those who have died will be regenerated from the indestructible memory of their spirit.

If you recall when I was talking about glands and our endocrine system as being the connection point between the seen and the unseen aspects of ourselves, I will take it one step further by pointing to the relation between how we think and feel, and "how we look".

From the limited scientific knowledge we possess of the nature of our consciousness and how it interacts with our body, we know that glands are activated to produce biochemical messengers by unseen thought impulses or emotions. These biochemical messengers (information) travel through the nervous system to trigger the movement and creation of things in our body. These signals are electrical, not unlike the signals that travel through electrical or telecommunication networks. And we are able to measure the amount of voltage we produce. In Chinese medicine, these circuits, or energy pathways, are known as meridians. And they have long been known to act as the way the mind communicates with the body, and vice versa. Any disruption of the information going down these pathways will create an imbalance in our health.

Although electricity is invisible, we know it is real because we can create it, direct it, and measure it. And of course, we can die from being shocked by it. So although we can't see the electricity that runs through us, we know it is clearly there.

Now, also realize this, that we are "light beings" from the point of view of physics and biochemistry. In fact, all of life on this planet is dependent upon the Sun for their biological processes. It was years ago that I watched an episode of the television science program, *The Nature of Things*, hosted by David Suzuki, and he was pointing this out. He was saying that whenever we eat something, we're actually eating photons—light particles emitted by the Sun, which our body then incorporates into building protein—flesh, skin, blood, bones—and also converting it into energy. And that when something such as a tree burns, the fire releases the trapped light energy back into the universe.

The process of plant photosynthesis is the main vehicle by which the Sun's energy is absorbed and converted. So when we eat plants, we're eating bits of the Sun. And when we eat animal meat, we're also indirectly consuming light energy.

If we could put on a special pair of goggles that could shift our vision to see the electrical currents and light energy that our body emits, I think we'd be looking at a layer of us that is purely energy. Some would even say we'd be looking directly at *spirit*.

I see this bio-electric light energy as an energy field that both surrounds us, and penetrates us; and all of our thoughts, feelings and organic processes create the size and intensity of this field. What I'm getting at here is that there is a basis to show that we are much more than what we see with our eyes, or feel with our finger tips. We are a fusion of different layers of energy, and there is an order, and permanence, to it all. And we know from the laws of thermodynamics, that energy cannot be created or destroyed, only converted from one form to another.

At a microbiological level, our genetic material—deoxyribonucleic acid (DNA)—is the blueprint from which all the structure of our body is built, and through which flows our soul, our essence, and personality. But understand this. Our DNA is not the ultimate source of what we are; rather it is the builder, and the conduit which receives instructions from a higher energetic level, the level of spirit energy. This is the dimension where our architectural plan, or blueprint, exists. Some would call it our "Spiritual DNA." For just as our thought and emotional impulses trigger the manifestation of molecules, so too our Spiritual DNA orchestrates the function of our molecular DNA. Our source is pure spirit.

I have often conceptualized Jesus' transfiguration as "turning up the volume" of the bioelectric/light field, to the point that light and matter became indistinguishable from each other. But even this visualization is a very weak and inadequate description of the glory of what occurred, and which we have all inherited by His sacrifice.

THE GRAVE AND "AWAKENING"

So, if we are dead and "asleep," what happens to our spirit? Our consciousness ceases and who we were remains in "God's memory." We will be regenerated, just as we appeared the first time when we entered this world, when our spirit emerged from the heart of God. In other words, our spirit doesn't fly to heaven, and doesn't remain in conscious limbo waiting for the Second Coming. It simply becomes unmanifest, like switching a light off. When we are re-animated, the light will be turned back on, and our former image will be reconstituted, "spiritual brick, by spiritual brick" by the power of the Holy Spirit.

My conception of what we'll look like when we come back to life is the healthiest, happiest condition we had while we lived. And any disfigurement or illnesses we may have been burdened with will disappear. We will exist in the most perfect, radiant form imaginable. And it will not matter what condition, or where our "remains" may be—be they in a mausoleum, or as ashes having been scattered upon the river of our childhood. Our spiritual essence will be awakened from its slumber when Christ comes back. And as to those who do not accept Jesus, the Gospels tell us they shall be extinguished, once and for all, and thus remain eternally separated from God.

CHAPTER SIX

The Divide between Spirituality and Religion

"But if you can do anything [to heal our son], take
pity on us and help us!"
    And Jesus said to him, "If You can!" All things
are possible to him who believes" (Mark 9: 22-23).

There are countless people who were born and raised in
Christianity, but who have stopped believing in Christ.
And not going to Church isn't the whole reason. Just because
one goes to Church or Mass every Sunday, does not mean
they are spiritual. That is, they may go through the routine
of following along in the worship ceremony, but they engage
with their head. To be spiritual is to engage with the heart,
to feel that you are a beloved child of God with a purpose
for your existence. That no matter where you may be, you are
already walking in faithfulness, thanksgiving, and complete
dependence upon Jesus for your guidance. Your private prayer
place, and even your own body, is your Church. And when you
pray, you do so intimately with Christ, knowing that you are
being listened to, rather than praying in public for the sole

purpose of appearing to be holy and righteous so you can gain favor with men and women.

To be spiritual is to value the meaning of the words, rather than their repetitive dogma. It means "becoming invisible" in the eyes of others—to perpetually be in a state of simplicity and radical humility no matter what your degree of success is. It is about the state of your soul that you bring to worship and not the fancy clothes or expensive jewellery you want to distract your fellow Churchgoers with.

For those of you who have strayed away from your faith in Christ, or never had it in the first place, begin to read the Gospels, and let Jesus' words and deeds sink into your heart. You will not only realize His strength of persona, but the power you can harness by following Him. Make Jesus the strong foundation of your life and ask the Holy Spirit to work within you for discernment and understanding, remembering what Jesus said,

> "But the Helper, the Holy Spirit, whom the Father will send in My name, He will teach you all things, and bring to your remembrance all that I said to you" (John 14: 26).

THE FORCES OUTSIDE OF US

So often people have asked me, "Is evil a real, supernatural force, like in the sense that Satan and his demons exist, or is evil just a human metaphor to explain things that we find hurtful?"

As I write these words, I have just been made aware that serial killer, Clifford Olson, has died of cancer in prison at the age of seventy-one. He was the notorious child and young adult murderer who terrorized the West Coast of Canada in the early 1980s. And even until the day he died, he showed no pity or remorse for what he had done. Psychiatrists have rationalized that he was simply a sociopath who was likely born with his deviant instincts, that his brain wiring was different from that of the average, decent, person.

But there is something much more going on at a spiritual dimension, for Jesus Himself taught us that there are very real forces of darkness that are always trying to find an opening into our hearts and minds. Deliverance was a crucial part of Christ's ministry. He not only healed people of their physical afflictions, but rebuked, and drove demons from them as well.

THE REALITY OF SATAN

We must understand this. Just as you and I are real, and know that we exist, so do Satan and his demons. He is known by multiple names in the Bible, such as Lucifer, Beelzebul, the adversary, the devil, and the god of this world. He was a powerful angel who led a rebellion against God in heaven, and was cast out together with one third of all the angels, those who had joined him. Satan is the god of all that is dark and evil in this world. The domain of suffering and separation from God is his spiritual kingdom.

However, we shouldn't live in fear and be worried about being attacked at every turn, rather we are to be vigilant of how we conduct our lives, to keep our heart and deeds clean, honest, and free from sin, and trust in Christ always, for those who follow and call to Him will be delivered from oppression. And He comforted us by saying,

> "These things I have spoken to you, that in me you may have peace. In the world you have tribulation, but take courage; I have overcome the world" (John 16: 33).

We need to be mindful of how we feed our souls. We can either consume the lies and deception of the god of this world (and live through our false self), or we can feed our being with the word of God.

The more we read the Bible and devote ourselves to applying what Jesus asked of us, the more we'll purify our subconscious awareness and strengthen our conscious shields of perception to distinguish right from wrong. We will seek to do what is truthful and lawful, and not what is convenient, selfish and self-serving. For whenever we act in our own self-interest, to the detriment of our neighbor, we are strengthening the forces of darkness, of ignorance.

Jesus warned us to resist temptation, and to pray for guidance. Even the Lord's Prayer says, "Lead us not into temptation, but deliver us from evil." I believe the more we wander away from our sense of self and our faith in Jesus, we can begin to open ourselves up to fear and ungodly distractions. And the more we live in a state of self-glorification, we literally begin to undergo a physical transformation, especially in how our brain begins to mold itself. As we think and act, so we end up becoming.

Brain science has shown that our brain is very "plastic," or malleable, and that the more we think in a certain way, neurons and brain cells begin to form structure, and connections which will preserve these thoughts—building new wiring—and hence, construct enduring behaviors in us. This is no more evident than what happens to people who become addicted to drugs. Their brain chemistry is radically different from that of the average person. And so it becomes so much more difficult to undo the damage that "the opening up the door to demons" has done.

And we are seeing that people who are obsessed with anything, be it sugar, sex, exercise, gambling, the Internet, and so on, have noticeable brain differences. This is not to say that all pleasurable pursuits are wrong, only when they begin to interfere with our overall health and relations with others; when they turn into uncontrolled addictions.

In His parable of the sower, Jesus demonstrates that we must continually set our thoughts to His words lest we become deceived by Satan:

> "And He answered and said [to His disciples],
> "The one who sows the good seed is the Son of Man, and the field is the world; and *as for* the good seed, these are the sons of the kingdom; and the tares [weeds] are the sons of the evil one; and the enemy who sowed them is the devil, and the harvest is the end of the age; and the reapers are angels.
> Therefore just as the tares are gathered up and burned with fire, so shall it be at the end of the age.
> The Son of Man will send forth His angels, and they will gather out of His kingdom all stumbling blocks and those who commit lawlessness, and will cast them into the furnace of fire; in that place there shall be weeping and gnashing of teeth" (Matthew 13: 37-42).

A key to prevent us from being deceived by Satan is to always live in truth. We have all heard the saying "The truth will set you free." And this is no more evident than when we confront the hurt part of ourselves and expose it to the light of day. We can live our whole life in torment (and thus gratify the devil) by ignoring the issues of our heart. We must pray into the source of our wound and ask Jesus to restore us and deliver us from our pain. Ask Him to clear your mind of the temptations and negative thoughts that are demonizing you.

But we must remember to do our part. We need to honestly look in the mirror and examine the wound, forgive ourselves, or forgive those who may have injured us. If you are harboring ill will and revenge, pray that these energies will be cast out and replaced with love and acceptance instead. Stop holding on to the things that no longer serve you, and allow yourself to shed them off, and be done with them.

Despite what your egoic mind may try to assure you of, remember that the devil doesn't have your best interests in mind. He wants to rob you of your future, and destroy your health and happiness. Whenever temptation arises, and you are struggling with overcoming it, or can't understand where it is coming from, pray to Jesus to reveal the truth and root of your suffering, and make Him the Lord of all your thoughts and actions.

Too many people have I known that have been plagued by various demons of chronic illness or addiction. "Gerald," a former co-worker of mine in the oil and gas sector, had been an alcoholic and hadn't had a drink in years, and yet he was deeply sad on the inside despite everything that came out of his mouth saying otherwise.

One day, I finally asked him if he was happy. And he stared at me, dumbfounded, and exclaimed, "Of course I'm happy! I've got a wonderful woman, a high-paying job that lets me play golf wherever I want, I have the house of my dreams, and I can eat whatever I like. Isn't that all there is to being happy?"

I replied, "Is it?"

Amazingly, his expression changed, and he frowned and said, "No." His heart knew better, and was far wiser than his egoic mind which was trying to keep up the pretence.

It so happened that he came from a wealthy family, but was constantly trying to prove to his father that he too could be a self-made man of material prosperity. Not only was there rivalry in his growing up, but deep-seated bitterness and resentment towards his father for having placed so much pressure on him to "not be a loser." So although he was supposedly a "winner" on the outside because he had all the best stuff money could buy, and which he could show off to his Alberta oil industry buddies, his soul paid a very heavy price of daily, internal poverty.

He had been deceived by the god of this world by not listening to his true self. Gerald was an atheist, and stubborn to the bone when it came to changing his ways, and I knew it wasn't my place to convert him, or tell him what he needed to do, unless he asked me to. And so I prayed for him, hoping the demons he was choosing to hold onto would be released, and that he would find peace.

HAVING JESUS IN YOUR LIFE

"Lindsey," a female friend and former co-worker of mine was looking for "more" in her life but wasn't sure what that was. And the subject of death terrified her, and it was something she simply couldn't confront. It was, in fact, at the root of her inability to have deep, meaningful relationships. Her insecurity was not only unattractive, but drove potential life partners away from her, like the opposite effect of lions being attracted to the scent of fear in the wild.

Whenever I'd be in her office discussing work items, our conversation would end up veering toward religion. She went to a Catholic school when growing up, and said she was raised as a "good little Catholic girl," but that she never really ended up believing in Jesus, nor that there was a God. Yet she lamented the fact that her two young sons wouldn't have the same sense of happiness that I had. But she affirmed that she would never voluntarily introduce them to Jesus, because it would be as misleading as telling them that Santa Claus, the Tooth Fairy, and the Easter Bunny were real.

I could hardly contain my laughter because she wasn't joking—she was absolutely serious. But then she went on to say that if only she could receive *personal* proof of the supernatural, then she would likely become a believer. Hearing this, I smiled, remembering the line from the movie, *Contact,* starring Jodie Foster as Ellie Arroway, a woman of science in search of extra-terrestrial life, and Matthew McConaughey playing the role of Palmer Joss, a preacher, a man of God. In one scene, Ellie said she would need proof of a supernatural, higher intelligence—God—before she would become a believer. And

Palmer said something like this, "Your father, did you love him?" And Ellie replied, "Of course I did." And Palmer said, "Prove it." She was perplexed, because she could not do so in the scientific, empirical way that she was used to.

So, I took the opportunity to use the same line on Lindsey, being fully mindful that I was definitely no Palmer Joss. I asked her if she loved her boys (she wasn't married and had no man in her life), and she of course said she did. So I asked her to prove it. She shook her head in confusion and said, "Well, I tell them that I love them every morning before sending them off to school, and I buy them whatever they need, and we just got back from a trip to Mexico." But she knew that this really wasn't proof, because love is an internal, personal relationship that cannot be proven to anyone.

She then moved on to what it meant to be a good person. And she said she didn't need to read anything, or be inspired by anyone, let alone Jesus, in order to be a good person (and yet I had never mentioned Jesus in all the chats I had with her). And for this reason she didn't need any spirituality. She affirmed, "I know when I'm doing things that are right, versus when I'm doing things that hurt others, because my conscience tells me so."

I asked her what she meant by her "conscience." She fumbled and said she couldn't explain what it *was*, only that is was how she felt. *That's good,* I thought to myself. *She's beginning to acknowledge the importance of her spirit.*

After that, whenever I'd walk past her office, she'd look up at me from her desk, and I could see that she wanted to ask me something. And I realized that something was changing inside of her. But I would just say a quick hello, and keep on my way, letting the Holy Spirit work in her heart so she could discover things in her own time.

Believing in Christ is not something we just do once. We must continually do what He taught us to, with a willing attitude:

"And why do you call Me, 'Lord, Lord,' and do not
do what I say?" (Luke 6: 46).

THOSE THINGS THAT ARE IMPOSSIBLE WITH MAN,
ARE POSSIBLE WITH GOD

I will admit that I have not paid enough attention to
Christ's declaration:

> "Truly, truly, I say to you, he who believes in Me, the
> works that I do shall he do also; and greater *works*
> than these shall he do; because I go to the Father"
> (John 14: 12).

What exactly did He mean by this? That we could
supernaturally walk on water, calm the storm, or heal the deaf
and the blind with a touch? I see this as another of Christ's
encouragements and challenges for us to stop doubting
ourselves and the unlimited abundance of God.

He wanted us to break out of the mold of our old ways
of thinking, that of doubt and limitation, and to push the
boundaries of our potential. And although I haven't attempted
walking on water, how can I say that the miracles of the past
are not occurring each and every day, in every part of the
world? What are we to say about those who have recovered
their vision from blindness, or a woman who was finally able
to conceive a child despite all the medical claims that it was
impossible? If we have been promised to be restored back to
life from death, with eternal, glorified bodies, then I'd like to
think that anything is possible for us if we have faith.

For many of us, we set our sights on things that are easy
to obtain, and then settle for a less than fulfilling life, and end
up living in regret. We need to push the boundaries of our
expectations, and dream big, knowing that God has a large
destiny for us to claim. And in spite of the obstacles that may

confront us, or all the past failures we've had, remember that Jesus will guide us and be with us in the boat of our quest. Take courage and put out into the deep, for your harvest will be great:

> "And when He had finished speaking, He said to Simon,
>
> "Put out into the deep water and let down your nets for a catch."
>
> And Simon answered and said, "Master, we worked hard all night and caught nothing, but at your bidding I will let down the nets."
>
> And when they had done this, they enclosed a great quantity of fish[.]" (Luke 5: 4-6).

CHAPTER SEVEN

Stress and Joy

"It is the Spirit who gives life; the flesh profits nothing; the words that I have spoken to you are spirit and are life" (John 6: 63).

Jesus doesn't want us to live in a state of stress. We are to live in a constant state of joy! Stress is the great malady of our times. In fact, we have been endlessly reminded that we live in "*the* age of stress," and medical professionals are always emphasizing that *all* of our diseases arise from stress—emotional, and physical.

Stress is a fact of life we're told, and that's why everywhere we look, we're being given advice on how to manage it. Just examine your Internet home page, and you'll likely see a new article about stress management being posted once a week. Self-help books tell you they've got your solution on how to deal with it. Sadly, the ocean of advice that's out there almost exclusively deals with handling the *symptoms* of stress, rather than the source of it.

Stress in its basic form is when we are pushed outside of our normal physical and emotional boundaries. The steel cables that are designed to support and pull the weight of an elevator car are made to handle stress. However, if they are subjected to more weight than they were made to handle, they will snap.

The fight-or-flight response is an ancient mechanism that we have inherited in order to protect us from *physical* harm. Unfortunately, this response is constantly being turned on and used even when it's not really needed. For most of us, it is literally jammed, which then wears out our nervous system, and frays our emotional wellbeing.

Our adrenal glands, which sit atop our kidneys, are activated to produce a host of stress hormones, such as adrenalin, and cortisol, to trigger our body into preparing its energy reserves and muscles to prepare for some type of threat, such as attacks from other people, animals, to run from natural disasters, or survive without food and water for an extended period of time. These built-in survival mechanisms helped our ancestors survive, and are still very much relevant today. Surgically removing your adrenal glands will certainly remove all stress from your life, but it will also kill you. We need them to survive.

We live in a far more complicated world than our forebears—we are bombarded by stimuli (sounds, movements, lights) in our environment, and we can react defensively and emotionally more than we should, which can trigger the production of stress molecules, which in large enough quantities over a sustained period of time, can "poison" us—make us very tired, and ill, if not altogether depressed.

I was watching the evening news and they commented that a science study has shown that city dwellers are far more stressed than people who live in the country. *Gosh, what a revelation*, I sarcastically mused. Although we may not be consciously aware of all the stimuli that are surrounding us every second, our subconscious is working and reacting to them. And every call or email we receive stimulates our attention further. In all, our adrenal glands are steadily sending out stress hormones to defend our body, and give the necessary boost of energy to power our concentration. And like anything, too much of anything can deplete us.

I'm not advocating an anti-urban revolution here, because there are a great many of us who enjoy, and thrive, living in a city. Their level of stress may be manageable, and doesn't impair their health. But I'd bet anything that staying in touch with nature factors in to their lives, be it a walk along a river, or feeding the ducks at the local park. Country living, with its slower pace, generally provides less of a constant stream of stimuli for us to react to, and coupled with fresher air, and greater contact with nature, our body feels more at home, and at peace.

As I mentioned earlier, the news of teen, and even pre-teen suicides is alarming, and there is growing awareness that we need to focus more time and energy towards understanding and preventing it. Bullying and social isolation has always existed, but it seems to be far more wide-ranging, and there are more weapons available to the abuser to inflict harm, especially with the case of social media. I believe the pressures on our youth to "fit in" are greater than ever. When I was going to school, no one had cell phones, and the Internet was still years away. The only pressure we had was to try and have the latest fashions. But now, you've got to look right *and* have the latest technological devices to be accepted.

And so the pressure to have "stuff" begins to press in on us, and we begin to worry. Worry is the mind's trigger to activate our adrenal glands, the fight-or-flight response. Cortisol, in particular, is great at wreaking havoc with our brain chemistry by disrupting and interfering with the chemical messengers our brain uses to think clearly, and to stay calm.

Over time, we not only begin to feel unwell, experiencing such symptoms as headaches, "brain fog," insomnia, and fatigue, but also a lack of interest in things we should enjoy, and feeling unusually anxious all of the time. So the popular "cure" is to exercise, and to meditate. All well and good, but again, we are dealing with only the symptoms of stress. We need to get right to the root of the problem.

Where the cause of our stress is emotional, we need to discover the nature of the heart wound that remains unhealed. From my own experience, I've found that when I no longer enjoyed doing something, or didn't like being around certain people, I could sense it in my body. The body is very intelligent, and perceives things at a higher level than the intellect. And it is the great medium through which our soul communicates with us—in our feelings and emotions. So listen to it. Listen to the aches you get in your gut, your chest, and your joints.

When you bang your knee against the coffee table, you'll definitely notice, and likely put some ice on the sore as soon as possible to reduce any swelling and bruising. If you end up getting a case of food poisoning, you should seek medical attention, and be aware of what you ate that made you sick. In other words, we seem to be very good at reacting to, and treating, physical stresses, but not so good at tending to the emotional and spiritual ones. These hidden aches need special attention, because they can hide for years like an iceberg conceals its true size beneath the waterline.

This is where we bring in Jesus. Pray to Him to show you the source of your discomfort. Invite the Holy Spirit in to bring it to the surface. Be kind to yourself, and be patient. Continually, and gently, place your awareness in your heart, and your belly. Ask Jesus why you feel unhappy, and wait for an answer; then shift your feelings to those things that you truly enjoy doing. Visualize them, and feel yourself doing them. Plug your happiness back in. And above all put your mind at peace, for Jesus reminded us to not worry about *anything*:

> "I say to you, do not be anxious for *your* life, *as to* what you shall eat, nor for your body, *as to* what you shall put on. For life is more than food, and the body than clothing" (Luke 12: 22).

And,

> " . . . which of you by being anxious can add a *single* cubit to his life's span?" (Luke 12: 25).

And,

> "For where your treasure is, there will your heart be also" (Luke 12: 34).

The concern I have about those who are seeking help, is their dependence on superficial treatments, or band-aid solutions, to their stress and anxiety, which may only serve to prolong, if not cause their situation to become worse. I've seen how self-help gurus promote meditation as a cure-all. Deep breathing and stillness have certainly been shown to work on the vagus nerve, activating the parasympathetic nervous system like applying the brakes to the adrenal glands. And when the adrenals stop producing stress hormones, the body can then begin to relax. And when the body is at peace, the mind will be at peace. But great as this may be, *temporarily* relaxing the mind and body will not solve the underlying issues we may have.

Deep breathing and cognitive (thinking) techniques have also been employed to cope with anxiety or panic attacks. A panic attack is an extreme physiological response to a stressor, and it is characterized with a sense of losing control of your mind or your body, usually accompanied by chest pain as if you're having a heart attack with a rapid heart rate, sweating, and shaking. These reactions are not life-threatening; they are essentially a "false alarm," an overreaction, and do pass. But the experience can leave the person extremely agitated and fearful that it will reoccur, and that they won't know what to do if, or when, it comes back.

All the breathing techniques and "mind tricks" (like confronting the fears, or counting backwards) you can employ are merely scratching the surface of the problem, much like taking cold medication to treat your stuffy, runny nose.

Being in a constant state of nervousness, and experiencing anxiety attacks, are signs of a much deeper issue that must be addressed, for they can be part of, or lead to, a state of depression (the emperor of all illnesses), a level of energy where the joy of our soul becomes buried, imprisoned. These conditions, in my opinion, are the result of emotional, physical, and mental fatigue or burnout. We need to attack this exhaustion, to re-establish *permanent* peace and rest.

We need to give all of our fears and burdens to Jesus, and talk to our family, friends, and the vast medical and social establishment that we are fortunate to have around us. Tackling this should always be a team approach, with Jesus at the lead, for He is the source of our permanent peace. I'm not of the belief, like some radical Christians, that we should turn away medical help and *only* pray. Yes, we need to use prayer as our first response to a crisis, but God has blessed the world with caring people who are here to assist us. So never hesitate to ask for help.

For all who are suffering in silence because of the pressures that you are facing, or the addictions that are gripping you, know always that Jesus loves you, and is always there to mend your broken heart. Call to Him, and He will answer. The Lord is your Shepherd who will show you the way out. He will allow you to lie down in green pastures, lead you beside quiet waters, and restore your soul (see Psalm 23).

When you no longer enjoy what you are doing, don't ignore that feeling. Listen to it, and move to a place where you can do what you love, and are good at. Don't be so busy filling your time with clutter that you choke out your personal sense of control and peace of mind. That is, don't take on more than you can handle. Don't think you're Superman or Supergirl, and don't do things to simply gain acceptance or favor from others. The only favor you need to gain is with Jesus.

Maintain a healthy balance in your life that incorporates your devotion to Christ, your family, your work, your friends, your community, and of course, the nourishment of your own body, mind, and soul.

Sometimes we need to go deep on certain heart wounds we're dealing with. Some require more prayer, time and patience to overcome:

> "But this kind [of affliction] does not go out except by prayer and fasting" (Matthew 17: 21).

And if we possess the personal strength, it might be best to go through the process so that we can become more resilient. And I don't mean this in the sense to deliberately set out to submit ourselves to pain and suffering, but when we find ourselves there, to have faith that it shall pass, and that we may be able to learn a fundamental lesson which we can then build into our lives. And when we see the storm clouds approaching in the future, be it in our own lives, or those who are close to us, we can effectively handle it and "rebuke" it.

"GOOD STRESS"—GROWING STRONGER IN THE SPIRIT

Now after this lengthy discussion of the negative effects of stress, I'm going to turn things on their head, and say that stress is not our enemy. It is something that we can harness to become stronger in our actions and faith.

If we didn't experience stress, we wouldn't be able to get up in the morning, or go to work, or have the concentration necessary to perform the tasks we thrive at. In fact, without any stress, we'd be dead. But here, I'm talking about "good stress." You may be thinking that it's something like good and bad cholesterol. Well, yes, somewhat. Good stress is limited in duration, and has just the right amount of hormones that we need for focusing on tasks and overcoming worthwhile challenges, let alone keeping us safe from physical danger.

As leaders, and followers, we need to be able to draw on our coping mechanisms to handle the multiple stresses that face us, in such a way, that we don't become depleted, or altogether worn out. We were designed to handle certain amounts of pressure, some more than others. That is why we are called to different occupations—be it a surgeon, a firefighter, or a soldier. We are not all built equal. But as a whole, Christ wants us to each do our part to support the leaders in our life so they don't buckle and snap under the entire burden. In any organization you're a part of, be it the place you work, or with your family, you need to work as a team to succeed. That means everyone has got to carry their share of the load, and not simply heap all the chores upon a single individual.

We need to also realize that unless we face certain challenges, we can never take ourselves to a higher level. If we think something is far too hard or stressful to even try, our soul takes a back seat to the egoic mind, and Satan claps his hands in his own sense of delight for our failure.

Have you ever looked back on your life and been proud of having overcome difficulties, such as financial, or medical, and told yourself, "Had I not gone through that hard stuff, I wouldn't have ended up where I am and become a better person for it"? The fact is that we do acquire wisdom by pushing against our limits, and what we thought were barriers, or limitations, were largely illusions of fear planted by the adversary. We can then set our sights upon going even further, knowing what we have accomplished.

Believe it or not, you will be provided with all the necessary energy and guidance that you need for any noble challenge you undertake, because we were not placed on this earth to live in fear or doubt, but to be strong, vibrant, and free. See your pursuits not as obstacles, but as challenges to become a far greater individual than you could have ever imagined.

This lifetime of ours wasn't meant to be easy. We will be thrown some pretty tough tests. But it was meant to be full of victory and blessing, so long as we realize that Jesus is always with us. I am forever inspired by the passage that reminds us of Christ's presence in the storm:

> "And there arose a fierce gale of wind, and the waves were breaking over the boat so much that the boat was already filling up.
> And He Himself was in the stern, asleep on the cushion; and they awoke Him and said to Him, "Teacher, do You not care that we are perishing?"
> And being aroused, He rebuked the wind and said to the sea, "Hush, be still."
> And the wind died down and it became perfectly calm.
> And He said to them, "Why are you so timid? How is it you have no faith?"
> And they became very much afraid and said to one another,
> "Who then is this, that even the wind and the sea obey Him?" (Mark 4: 37-41).

No matter what stresses or hardships we are facing, we need only call to Jesus and ask for His help, for He will not allow our boat to sink in the storm. And in having a deep spiritual life in Christ, we are building internal resiliency of the soul that can better withstand the gales and waves of life that may buffet us along the journey.

STEPPING BEYOND SUFFERING

When I knocked at their door, it was already getting late on that August evening of 2001. But the sky was absolutely clear of clouds, and the moon and stars were brighter than I could ever recall.

I had an appointment with "Floyd" and "Martha" to lease their farm's petroleum and natural gas rights, just west of the village of Wardsville in Southwestern Ontario.

Martha opened the door, and she struck me as the typical older farm wife—she was of medium height, stocky in build, and was a no-nonsense woman. She invited me in to the kitchen where we could discuss the terms of the lease, and her husband, Floyd, was already seated at the table. I was momentarily stunned at what I saw—he was deathly pale (or rather, some shade of unknown yellow), and was emaciated, a mere toothpick beside the figure of his wife. He must have been in his late 60s or early 70s, and the impression I got was that he was gravely ill. I introduced myself, and I could barely feel any strength or warmth in his hand as I shook it.

"Don't mind Floyd, mister. He just got home from the hospital from his chemo treatments. He's still got cancer, but he's still ticking."

I went over the petroleum and natural gas lease and grant document with them, while being peppered with blunt questions from Martha, such as, "When you gonna drill an oil well, and how much we gonna be paid?" And, "How close will you come to the water well and the house?"

While I was talking with her, Floyd didn't ask a single question—he just smiled and stared at me the whole time. It wasn't in a strange way. It was like he was seeing with the eyes of a child, with complete joy and fascination, like appreciating the wonder of a butterfly, of life.

"Well, sounds good to me. Where do we sign?" Martha grunted. She scribbled her name on her signature line, and then gave the pen to Floyd, who wrote his own rather agilely and with ease for someone as ill as he was. When he was finished, he looked up at me and asked, "Do you know any history?"

Martha exclaimed, "Oh boy, here we go. Floyd, it's getting late, and this young man's gotta get home."

I looked at Floyd and felt compassion for him. I sensed he had maybe only weeks to live, and that he wanted to express his happiness for being alive through his interest of history.

"Actually, I majored in history while in university," I replied.

"Let me show you something, then." He got up and shuffled to the kitchen door and we walked outside. He pointed to his field, which was full of soybeans as far as the eye could see, the moonlight being reflected off of its carpet-like surface. "I'm always finding Indian stuff out there—arrow heads, spear points, and such. Did you know that the Shawnee chief Tecumseh and his Indian war party camped in this very field the night before he died at the Battle of the Thames during the War of 1812?"

"No, I didn't. That's remarkable." We were a quite far from the actual battle site and I didn't think he had his facts correct, but I decided it was best not to enter into an academic debate it over.

He continued, saying, "They had a large pow wow to prepare for their fight against the Americans from Detroit. And I've even had an archaeologist from London come out here and survey the grounds. He then whispered, "And sometimes, on a warm, clear summer night like we have tonight, I swear I can hear faint yelling, and drum beats, as well as see wisps of white dancing in a circle—ghosts."

He was ever so weak that he could barely stand, and I thought I'd have to prop him up a few times, but he was beaming—he seemed oblivious to his condition and was completely immersed in the mood of his story. It was like nothing in the universe mattered other than the happiness he was experiencing in the present moment. It was as if Floyd had transcended all stress, suffering, worry, and the fear of death—he had tapped into something eternal, into his passion.

Martha opened the door and yelled, "Floyd, for heaven's sake, let the young man go home, and get in the house!"

Floyd kept on talking as if she didn't exist. I sensed he was truly grateful to have someone to talk to, someone to listen to him. I felt it was the very least I could do, and also because I was aware that I was learning something very important, and it wasn't just the local history lesson. As I drove away, down his gravel driveway, Floyd waved and stared at me until I could no longer see him in my rear-view mirror.

ACCEPTANCE AND BELONGING

Several years ago when I was still living at home and attending university, I was driving past a low income housing complex, and while I was stopped at a red light, I observed a young family crossing the street in front of me. There was a young boy of about the age of six walking in front of his rather heavy and unkempt mother, who was pushing her infant daughter in a baby stroller. Although this family was noticeably poor, I sensed that the little boy was very content. He was skipping along, singing to himself ahead of his mom and baby sister, and I got the complete sense that he was happy because he felt secure, was accepted, and felt loved. He didn't appear to need anything else in the entire world.

So much pain and suffering is a result of rejection. This is no more evident than in a school setting when kids are bullied, excluded, and marginalized because they don't meet certain "standards." And where there is rejection there is no relationship. And where there is no relationship, there is no love.

The most important thing to nearly all of us is being accepted for what we are, and when we're not, we become hurt on the inside. We all want to be part of something, and be recognized on a first name basis, because we were made to be social creatures, to grow and interact with others, to discover the depths of our heart and humanity. And could we still be human if we never interacted with others? Relationship is what makes us who we are. As Jesus has accepted us, so we are commanded to love others:

> "By this all men will know that you are My disciples,
> if you have love for one another" (John 13: 35).

Rejection can really hurt, but Jesus experienced the same pain when His divinity was denied by His own townspeople of Nazareth, and of course, when He was crucified. This is why Christianity is alive and relevant, because Jesus is always seeking us out to establish, renew, or deepen our relationship with Him because he can personally identify with our suffering. This friendship gives us purpose, strength, and courage in life. He is the best friend we have ever had, or ever will have. For He even died for us so that the burden of our sins could be removed, thereby giving us the gift of eternal life:

> "Greater love has no one than this, that one lay
> down his life for his friends" (John 15: 13).

SOCIETAL SHIFT

I have hope for society when I see people coming forward with their heartrending stories of their loved ones having taken their own lives. The suffering that has been contained in the shadows is being exposed to the light of day, and people are beginning to understand that, more and more, we are all becoming personally impacted by violence towards one another, be it verbal abuse in the school yard, or the physical injuries sustained on the football field, in the boxing ring, or in the hockey arena. The days of fighting, or being a "tough guy" is becoming less acceptable than it was a few short years ago.

The disease, Chronic Traumatic Encephalopathy (CTE) is fast becoming a household name. We are realizing that repeated head trauma, through punches to the head, or in concussions resulting from hitting the ice surface, turf, or other helmets, have progressive, destructive effects on the brain. This leads to pain, depression, and mental suffering of those afflicted, and we are seeing more incidents of current and former athletes committing suicide. And their families and friends are left to deal with the full force of this disease. If sports authorities make the necessary changes, there are ways to play competitively while minimizing the risks of severe injury. And when injuries do occur, full rehabilitation must be the priority before any return to the playing field. In the end, harm to the body can lead to the suffering of the soul.

HEAVEN ABOVE

"I and the Father are one" (John 10: 30).

Jesus instructed us to set our attention above, to heaven, for He reminded us that all that He did on earth was as the Father did in heaven. Christ is our connection to God and heaven, showing us that the same access is available to everyone. That is exactly right—even you! When we pray, we need to go to our secret place, to our imagination and feelings of the heart within, *and* where possible, to a physical place where we can be undisturbed:

> "But you, when you pray, go into your inner room, and when you have shut your door, pray to your Father who is in secret, and your Father who sees in secret will repay you"(Matthew 6: 6).

For Jesus Himself constantly stole away to pray in private:

> "And after He had sent the multitudes away, He went up to the mountain by Himself to pray; and

when it was evening, He was there alone" (Matthew 14: 23).

Our connection to God and His heavenly realm is often missed because our minds are too engaged in the steeplechase of our daily routine. That is why it is so crucial to take a time out from whatever we are doing, and place ourselves back in synch with the vibrations of our true self, and heaven. Prayer and meditation on Christ's words is like opening up the windows of your soul to allow the sunlight and rarefied air of heaven and the breath of the Holy Spirit in.

Jesus' connection to heaven allowed its unlimited power to manifest through Him, whether it was in feeding thousands with a handful of loaves and fishes, or healing the sick. And the power that flowed through Him was not only visible in its results, but palpable to the touch:

> "And all the multitude were trying to touch Him,
> for power was coming from Him and healing *them*
> all" (Luke 6: 19).

And we are reminded to always give thanks when we pray, because it shifts us into a state of humility where we're better able to receive, rather than in a state of arrogance, where we feel we are entitled to possess. And look up to heaven knowing that what you're seeking has already been granted to you. That is the way of heaven, that all that you need already exists. There is no lack of any kind there. For as in the Lord's Prayer, we are to seek on "earth as it is in heaven."

HAPPINESS—SERVING OTHERS

I don't know about you, but the greatest sense of happiness and satisfaction I get is when I serve others. I just feel good on the inside when I see their eyes light up and they smile and tell me, "Thank you." I briefly discussed the importance of service in Chapter One, but I am going to elaborate on it further, for I truly believe that this is our ultimate calling, to give our lives away in service to others.

Think back to a time when you assisted someone, either on the job or out in public. Aside from the fact that you gave someone something they needed (like a new insurance policy, or you opened a door for someone), did you not notice that it also validated who you were, and all the training, skills and good upbringing you were given? For we were not only created by God as survival machines, but as social beings. We were born to serve because service is a true reflection of the nature of our authentic self, and thus a reflection of Christ. When we act in selfishness, we are closing the door to our soul, and to each other. Selfishness is the domain of the egoic mind, ignorance, and the god of this world.

When we live in the belief that life is a competition for scarce resources, the spirit of service and cooperation shrivels. We must always ask ourselves how our desires and skills can be used to help and to serve others before we think of the compensation for what we'll do. When we act with the right attitude of placing our neighbor first, the reward will follow.

Beyond everything that Jesus came to do for us, He came to serve us, and to be the example of how we are to serve others. In the Gospel of John, it was Jesus who washed the feet of His disciples after the Passover Supper, which shocked them, especially Simon Peter:

> "And so He came to Simon Peter. He said to Him, "Lord, do You wash my feet?"
>
> Jesus answered and said to him, "What I do you do not realize now; but you shall understand hereafter" (John 13: 6-7).

Jesus' entire ministry was one of love and service. His teachings, His healings, and His crucifixion and death were all done for our benefit so that we could enter the kingdom of God—He didn't do it for fame, power, or wealth. He gave His life away in total service so that His only reward was to free us all from captivity, and the power of the devil.

Let Jesus be your role model in doing great work. Don't listen to negative talk that there's no money in what you want to do, or you'll never succeed. Know that your work is being done for the higher purpose of service, and the glory of God:

> "If any one serves Me, let him follow Me; and where I am, there shall My servant also be; if any one serves Me, the Father will honor him" (John 12: 26).

Where you can, serve and perform acts of kindness anonymously. There is great power and benefit in this. For when good things come your way, you can be assured that heaven itself is mysteriously rewarding you in kind, and in greater measure, for those good deeds you did in secret.

Prior to my move to Alberta, I submitted an anonymous application nominating "Brenda," one of my workmates (from a Bank I was working part-time at) for that financial institution's yearly awards of excellence. I felt she was not only very professional in what she did, but that she went the extra mile when it came to serving both customers and colleagues. Although she didn't win the award, she was ecstatic that someone had been thinking about her and had appreciated her hard work. And somehow she discovered that I had been the one who had nominated her.

I later left the Bank so I could devote more time to my oil and gas consulting work, and I was really itching to go out West, to the Alberta Oil Patch, as it had always been a childhood dream of mine. However, although I was single at the time, I didn't have the necessary leverage to pack everything up and make such a large transition, leaving family and friends behind.

It so happened about a year and a half later, I bumped into Brenda at the grocery store, and without prompting her, she asked if I was still doing petroleum exploration, and asked if I'd ever thought of moving to Alberta where activity was booming at the time. I was surprised because I'd been thinking about it for several weeks, and I had actually prayed for "a sign" the day before so I could put my mind to rest on whether to go, or to stay. So here it was, the sign I had asked for. And I reflected that had I not recognized Brenda's service, I would not have been given this gift of guidance from her. The rest is, as they say, history. I sent my resumé to a professional placement service located in Calgary through the Internet, and within six hours I got a telephone interview with a large oil development company. I was then flown out to Calgary, interviewed in person, given the job, flown back home, sold my place in Lambeth in thirty hours, said goodbye to everyone (well, actually, "I'll see you all in a few years"), and drove across the country to start a new adventure. In serving others, we ultimately (and "miraculously") serve ourselves:

"Therefore whatever you want others to do for you,
do so for them[.]" (Matthew 7: 12).

HUMILITY

This is something most of us really need to work on because it is key to being a good servant. When we are truly humble, we step outside of the influence of our egoic mind and free up our energy to look at someone else's needs rather than our own. When we're in a state of humility, we feel more peaceful and at ease, because being proud, arrogant, and self-centered, requires a lot of energy to maintain. When I look at Christ's example of submission in following God's plan to the Cross,

I am indeed humbled. And this He said for those who will follow Him:

> "Come to Me, all who are weary and heavy laden,
> and I will give you rest.
> Take My yoke upon you, and learn from Me,
> for I am gentle and humble in heart[.]" (Matthew
> 11: 28-29).

I know for me, being meek has been a challenge and something I try to always be mindful of. I'd especially notice it when I was waiting in line, such as at the Bank or at the grocery checkout. I'd be continually judging others who were ahead of me for being too slow, and thinking, *Why did they buy so many groceries (and look at all that junk food!)?* And, *Why is the teller so relaxed and slow? Doesn't she know I'm here and I've got places to go and things to do? Standing in line is so below me,* and so on. In reality, I was putting myself in a state of unnecessary agitation because I wasn't enjoying the present moment. My head kept looking ahead, thinking, *I don't want to be here because this is fruitless. I want to fast forward to the future where I can do something enjoyable and productive.* So I convinced myself, *I've got to change my attitude here.* And I prayed to Jesus to imbue me with the Holy Spirit, to shift my perspective. And it's been working.

Just last week when I went to the local government office that handles driver's licensing and health cards, I found myself at the end of a very long line. In the past, I'd be saying to myself, "Wonderful, just what I needed." But now I saw this as an opportunity to practice radical humility and pour cold water on my pride. So I looked at everyone and thought to myself that they all had "better" things to do, and that we were all in the same boat. I appreciated the way the desk clerks were professionally carrying out their jobs, and how happy people were when they'd been served. I observed the man and woman behind me with their baby girl. She was probably no more than eight months old, and I could feel her father's love for her as he held her in his arms.

There was an older woman ahead of me who called out to the man who had just paid for his service, "Hey "Bob," you could have paid for me too." She obviously knew the man. He stared at her facetiously and said, "Oh! Had I known you were there, I would have paid for you too! I'm not cheap." I nearly died laughing. The next moment I realized it was my turn to be attended to. When I left, I wondered where all the time had gone. There had been no impatience, no judgment of others, no demanding for time to speed up, only humility, acceptance, and even happiness.

The first step we need to make is acknowledging our own faults and planting the intent within ourselves that we both want, and need, to change. And when we ask for strength of mind, and perseverance from Christ, we will see a major shift in how we see others. We can then fully open ourselves up to looking outward, rather than selfishly inward.

It recently struck me that the skills and abilities that I may have are not ones that *I* put in *me*—I was born with them. So what right do I have to brag about any of my talents and accomplishments? The answer is absolutely none. God could have decided to give me nothing, and that's quite humbling to think of. And we are reminded in John 3:27, that "A man can receive nothing, unless it has been given him from heaven."

I was given the heart, mind, and body that I have to manifest God's glory into the world. And like any relationship, we need to reciprocate in our gift-giving. When was the last time you sent a Christmas card to someone during the holidays, and didn't receive one in kind from them? You probably made a mental note to not send them one the following year. So with us, God expects us to give back to Him by giving to others. Donate money, give your time, and give your attention to others. Serve them in the best possible way that you can.

CHAPTER EIGHT

Thy Kingdom Come

"Not every one who says to Me, 'Lord, Lord,' will enter the kingdom of heaven; but he who does the will of My Father *who is in heaven*" (Matthew 7: 21).

In the Lord's Prayer many of us miss the meaning of "Thy kingdom come." This is what Jesus was proclaiming about the kingdom of heaven, or the kingdom of God, which He used interchangeably. As I mentioned earlier, to me, this is both a divine and a literal kingdom that will be ushered in when He comes again to rule as the King of Kings for all eternity. He will save the human race at the end of the age from destruction, and we shall evolve into new beings, of changed character and everlasting spiritual bodies.

Although I am versed in Bible prophecy, it is not something I devote much energy to. And, in fact, I cringe whenever I come across television evangelists telling people to repent "for the end is near," or they have a large chart detailing all the events of history that show that we're very close to Armageddon and Christ's Second Coming. All the predictions I've ever heard end up being completely wrong, and I often wonder how often these people of God twist the facts just to fit their own hypotheses, or the creed of their sect, like trying to jam a square peg through a round hole. If anything, we should take note of Jesus' account of His return, for He made it clear that we are to live our lives according to His will and His word, and that no one knows exactly when He's coming back:

> "But of that day and hour no one knows, not even the angels of heaven, nor the Son, but the Father alone" (Matthew 24: 36).

Therefore, we are once again directed back to ourselves, and the present moment.

I was saddened by the death yesterday of Steve Jobs, co-founder of Apple Inc. The news hit me in a way I didn't expect, just like the time I heard that "Superman"—Christopher Reeve—had died. A friend of mine noted that I got all choked up.

Despite his fame and fortune, he was not able to add any more time to his life, and lost his struggle with pancreatic cancer. Most of us have followed not only his revolutionary product launches of the last few years—the iPod music device, the iPhone, and iPad—which have all transformed the world we live in, but also his health challenges—he got thinner each time we saw him. And yet his life and death represent a mirror for us to look into, to remember that the time that has been gifted to us must be lived to the fullest, pursuing our passions right now, for we do not know when our time will be up. His 2005 Stanford University Commencement address echoes what Jesus wanted us to place our focus on—on the life that we have. I don't recall his entire speech, but Steve said something like, our time is limited, and not to waste it living someone else's dreams, that we need to listen to our intuition and follow our heart, for it always knows best.

DETOURS ON THE ROAD TO THE KINGDOM

"Put your desire out into the *Universe*, and what you seek will be manifested" (Common New Age saying).

I've read a lot of New Age literature as a means to see what was out there, and I always find it interesting how they avoid invoking the name of God. They'll use any other expression, but avoid giving the due to Him. And Jesus is quoted and referred to frequently, but not as the divine Son of God, but as a man like us, who was able to pull back the veil that separates the physical world we can see, and the realm of spirit. In other words, he was a mystic, a wizard, a shaman, who through his own personal quest, and with the guidance of beings from "the other side," discovered the true nature of life and death, and our purpose in the universe.

I've seen where authors have gone belief shopping to every faith under the Sun, and have formulated their own program that they believe will surely work for everyone else. But for those who have come to know Jesus, we are aware that He spoke with authority, and is the only guide we need to find out the reality of who we are and what our destiny is. He is the eternal Son of God, and did not need to go on any vision quest, pilgrimage, or inner journey of discovery to find out who He was. When we acknowledge this truth, our life becomes simpler, and we no longer have to waste our time looking for the next best thing, or the guru who has uncovered something that the last one missed.

While there are those who say there are many paths to God and heaven, and to understanding our true spiritual identity, I'd have to say that this is just another fallacy the adversary has thrown our way to cause us to get lost in a wilderness of superstition. Unlike other religious teachers, Jesus said He was divine and that His way was the *only* way to God and eternal life:

"Truly, truly, I say to you, he who hears My word, and believes Him who sent Me, has eternal life, and does not come into judgment, but has passed out of death into life" (John 5: 24).

Jesus' words are not just "feel good" statements, but promises of a reality that shall be.

THE NEXT STEP

I don't subscribe to the belief that the theory of evolution is totally wrong. I disagree both with atheistic scientists, and Fundamental Creationists who strictly adhere to the Book of Genesis. I believe that God's majesty has been revealed through the process of change. And we are able to observe the precision and brilliance of God's handiwork through the lens of science. For us to reject the gifts of the studies of history, anthropology, archeology, geology, and all of the sciences, would be to diminish God's designs. And for us to ignore the monumental discoveries of our intellect would be like making up our own system of mathematics and denying that two plus two equals four. And although we were created in God's image, it was not done instantaneously. We, like all of life on earth, have evolved—we have changed and transformed into our current form; our bodies and minds have changed over time. And we will undergo yet another shift when we are regenerated, or are living at the time of Christ's return, to possess luminous, incorruptible bodies.

Like any valuable creation, it is improved upon and perfected over time. Just look at the automobile, the computer, or the cell phone. They started from somewhere, and look how they've been continually improved upon. So too it has been, and will continue to be, with us.

You may be thinking, *then what about Adam and Eve, the first man and woman created by God, as described in the Book of Genesis?* I believe in the symbolic, theological, concept of a first man and woman who gave rise to the human race, as well as a *real* couple that possessed the first attributes that we can identify as being part of our own species, *Homo sapiens.* Their appearance started us on the road to who we currently are, beings with intelligence and civilization, with all the joys and ills that that all entails. And this in no way takes away from the reality that God created people. We are all here, and we know that we came from our parents, and they from their parents, all the way back to Adam and Eve.

Jesus taught us to be discerning, to use the power of our intellect to ask questions, to be critical, and to always seek out the truth, rather than subscribe to religious doctrine:

> "Now no one after lighting a lamp covers it over with a container, or puts it under a bed; but he puts it on a lampstand, in order that those who come in may see the light.
>
> For nothing is hidden that shall not become evident, nor *anything* secret that shall not be known and come to light" (Luke 8:16-17).

In a way, this is also a challenge to those who don't believe in Jesus. He is essentially saying that everything He has said and done, if true, will be revealed to be true. And if false, then will be discovered to be false.

For those who believe there can never be a future divine kingdom that Christ has assured us of, what are they to say about the nature of the complexity of our own existing national governments? Did we not start off as hunters, gatherers, and pastoralists, who then settled down into villages, and began domesticating plants and animals on a full-time basis? Society then became more complex, and we began living in dense population centers—cities—like ancient Babylon, and all those other legendary place names from the Bible. Expansion of trade networks and the evolution of industry and technology followed along at a rapid pace thereafter.

Like our own predestined transition into a new life form, our way of life and how we are ordered will also evolve into the divine arrangement of the kingdom of God. Even utopians and humanists who do not believe in Jesus or the Father, predict that one day, our human ignorance will disappear, and we will enter a phase of world peace and harmony; a time when humanity will look back at its primitive and brutal ways that perpetuated war and suffering. It is only natural, they believe, that the next stage in our evolution will be one of enhanced morality and living in balance with all of life. It seems that such idealists are closer in ideology to the good news of the kingdom of heaven than they realize.

We do need to be aware that prophecy was a pillar of Jesus' ministry, and that our future resurrection and acceptance into the kingdom of heaven is prophetic. But we also need to stop worrying about the future, or engaging in a trivial pursuit of trying to decipher the Gospels and the Book of Revelation, thinking that we'll discover something someone has overlooked, or found the hidden code to one of Jesus' sayings. Stop wasting your energies on all this stuff, and place your time and attention upon all the people you encounter on a daily basis. Besides, do we not already have enough in our lives to burden us? Our job is simple. We need to foster a good heart, and leave the prophetic things for Jesus to handle. And whenever I'm in doubt of something, or find conflicting views concerning my faith, I remember to always go to my source, to my guide, and I remind myself, *If Jesus said it, then that's good enough for me.*

AFTERWORD

"And He was saying, "The kingdom of God is like a man who casts seed upon the ground; and goes to bed at night and gets up by day, and the seed sprouts up and grows—how, he himself does not know.

The earth produces crops by itself; first the blade, then the head, then the mature grain in the head.

But when the crop permits, he immediately puts in the sickle, because the harvest has come" (Mark 4: 26-29).

Like the sower of this parable, I too do not know the invisible workings of the Holy Spirit, but I know that following Christ has lead to a bountiful harvest of the heart for me.

If you were to ask me what the most important aspect of my faith in Jesus is, I'd have to say it is my relationship with Him. While I live in hope that I shall live for all eternity because of my belief in Him, this life is all I can claim certainty of—the Hereafter is in His hands. So while I'm here in this body, it is reassuring that someone has laid out a plan for me to live at the highest level possible, and moreover, that I can finally stop wandering spiritually, knowing that I have truly found my guide on the path of life.

It is so easy to get discouraged, distracted, and forgetful that Jesus is only but a thought or a feeling away, because the world we live in is like that. It causes us to have amnesia as to who we really are, and why we're here.

We belong to a divine family—all of us. And realizing our extraordinary nature is the first step to living up to our unlimited potential. Believing in Jesus allows us to unlock the many questions that have been with us from the beginning, and to bring lasting peace into our lives.

ABOUT THE AUTHOR

Nelson Mendes is a writer who has spent most of his life in pursuit of truth, has studied the many religions of the world, and has travelled to foreign places to broaden his horizons of God's Creation. He is also the author of *From Lusitania*, and was born in London, Ontario, Canada.

CPSIA information can be obtained at www.ICGtesting.com
Printed in the USA
LVOW060220290212

270849LV00001B/16/P